THE ROLE OF ENTREPRENEURS IN BACKWARD AREAS

H. SADHAK

1989
DAYA PUBLISHING HOUSE
Delhi - 110006

© 1989 MANJUSHRI SADHAK
H. SADHAK (b. 1950-   )

ISBN 81-7035-058-1

HC
435.2
.S235
1989

All rights reserved with the publishers including the right to translate or to reproduce this book or parts thereof except for brief quotations in critical articles or reviews.

Published by: Anil Mittal for Daya Publishing House at 1302, Vaid Wada, Nai Sarak, Delhi - 110 006,
Laser Typesetting by Computer Codes, Delhi-110009 & Printed at D.K. Fine Art Press, Delhi

PRINTED IN INDIA

IN MEMORY OF

MY

REVERED FATHER

CONTENTS

LIST OF TABLES		vii
LIST OF FIGURES		ix
APPENDICES		xi
INTRODUCTION		xiii
1.	Role of Entrepreneurs in Industrial Development	1
2.	Changing Industrial Environment in India	15
3.	Institutional Efforts to Develop Entrepreneurship in India	47
4	First Generation Entrepreneurs : A Field Study	69
5.	Performance of First Generation Entrepreneurs	91
6.	Towards an Entrepreneurial Developing Society	109
	APPENDICES	141
	INDEX	177

LIST OF STATISTICAL TABLES

2.1.	Income, unemployment and poverty in India.	23
2.2.	Urbanisation, infrastructure and Industrial Development.	25
2.3.	Area and population under industrially backward districts.	27
2.4.	National product and per capita income.	31
2.5.	Annual growth rate of Indian Economy	32
2.6.	Gross Domestic product at factor cost by Industry of origin	33
2.7	Selected Growth indicators (Large Scale Industries).	36
2.8.	Selected Growth indicators (Small Scale Industries).	37
2.9.	Growth rate of industrial production.	38
2.10.	Profile of Public Enterprises in India.	39
4.1.	Areawise distribution Industrial units.	70
4.2.	Location of Sample Units.	71
4.3.	Organisation type of sample units.	71
4.4.	Frequency distribution of sample units according to size of project costs.	72
4.5.	Frequency distribution of sample units according to size of employment.	73
4.6.	Age composition of entrepreneurs.	74
4.7.	Educational back ground of entrepreneurs.	75
4.8.	Past experience of Entrepreneurs.	77
4.9.	Length of past experience.	77
4.10.	Factors effecting motivation of entrepreneurs.	79
4.11.	Family background of Entrepreneurs.	82
4.12.	Regional mobility of Entrepreneurs.	83
4.13.	Determinants of location decision.	86
4.14.	Areawise distribution of investment and employment in sample units.	88

LIST OF FIGURES

1. Major institutions engaged in EDP in India.   54
2. Factors influencing early death of entrepreneurship.   116
3. An integrated model of resource linked entrepreneurship and industrial development.   125
4. Management of Entrepreneurship Development.   127

APPENDICES

(i)	List of No Industry Districts/Notified less developed Districts eligible for concessional finance from All India Financial Institutions under Backward Area Development Scheme.	141
(ii)	Yearwise Gross National Product and Net National Product.	155
(iii)	Gross Domestic Product at Factor cost by industry of origin.	158
(iv)	Statewise assistance sanctioned by All India Financial Institutions.	161
(v)	Statewise assistance disbursed by All India Financial Institutions.	164
(vi)	Statewise assistance sanctioned by State Financial Corporations.	166
(vii)	Statewise assistance disbursed by State Financial Corporations.	168
(viii)	Statewise assistance sanctioned by State Industrial Development Corporations.	170
(ix)	Statewise assistance disbursed by State Industrial Development Corporations.	172
(x)	A statistical sketch of economy of India Uttar Pradesh and Maharashtra.	174

INTRODUCTION

Entrepreneurs, who have assumed the role of key performers in the process of economic development, industrialisation and social change during the period followed by Industrial Revolution, are called Cultural Heroes, Agent of social change etc. The have emerged as the integral component development and instrument of social change and the societies are in search of such agents. According to Peter Kibly[a] "the search for a 'missing component' in the growth process of under developed countries is now a long established tradition." In fact, the underdeveloped countries, ignoring the importance of this component (Entrepreneur), attempted to develop natural resources, capital formation and technology etc. It is only recently that they have widened their outlook to include 'Entrepreneurship' as the most important component rapid industrial development and economic progress.

India, which witnessed spectacular progress in handicrafts and village industries, witnessed gradual decline in prosperous village industries with the establishment of British Rule. Consequently local entrepreneurs were pushed back causing a set back to emergence of Indian entrepreneur class. However, establishment of factory system in 19th Century paved the way for emergence of modern entrepreneurial class in India and, in spite of adverse political and economic environment, a large number of Parsi, Marwari and Jain entrepreneurs came up during this period. The real thrust on the development of entrepreneurship in India came during post Independence period, when a number of measures under various Five Year Plans were initiated to remove the obstacles imposed during British period. Several policy measures were also initiated to create an atmosphere conducive to growth of industry and entre-

---

a. Peter Kibly: 'Entrepreneurship and Economic Development' The Free Press (1971) New York.

preneurship. As a result, new entrepreneurs have come up breaking the social and economic barriers.

Various aspects of emerging entrepreneurship in India have been discussed in several studies by the Indian and foreign authors. The important studies in the field of entrepreneurship by Indian authors are conducted by D.R. Gadgil[b], Phiroz B Medhora[c], Amalendu Guha[d], M.N. Srinivas[e], K.L. Sharma and Harnek Singh[f] and V.K. Agarwal[g].

The important studies on Indian Enrtrepreneurship are conducted by foreign authors like, Helen B Lamb[h], E.W.Nafziger[i], Harold A. Goul[j] etc. The studies of these eminent authors have thrown light on the type, class, caste, communities, motivation and other interest factors of entrepreneurship development in India. After independence, more particularly, since the beginning of 70's the concept of entrepreneurship development got a new dimension and perspective due to Government. policy of removal of regional imbalance through industrial development in backward regions. The policy, to develop backward regions, is passed on the instruments of incentives, subsidies and other locational assistance in backward regions. The aim is to induce outside investment and promote local entrepreneurship in backward regions. In addition to incentives and subsidies, efforts have been made by various Government and private agencies to identify and train potential entrepreneurs.

---

b. D.R. Gadgil: 'Origin of Modern Indian Business Class' Institute of Pacific Relations, New York, 1959.

c. Phiroz B Medhora: 'Entrepreneurship in India', Political Science, Quarterly 80, (Sept. 1965).

d. Amalendu Guha: Persi Seths and Entrepreneurs 1750-1850, Economic & Political Weekly, Nov. 1970.

e. N.N. Srinivas: 'Mobility in the Caste System in Structure and change in Indian Society' M. Senger and B.S. Cohn, Aldine Publishing Co. Chicago, 1968.

f. K.L. Sharma & Harnek Singh: 'Entrepreneurial Growth and Development Programme in North India,' Abhinava Publications, New Delhi, 1980.

g. V.K. Agarwal: 'Initiative Enterprise & Economic changes in India' Munshiram Manoharlal Publishers Pvt. Ltd., New Delhi, 1975.

h. Helen B. Lamb: The rise of Indian Business Community, Pacific Affairs (June 1955).

i. E.W. Nafziger: Class, Caste and Entrepreneurship, University Press of Hawaii (East West Centre), Honolulu, 1978.

j. Harold A. Goul: The adaptive Functions of Caste in Contemporary Indian Society, Asian Survey - 3 (Sept. 1963).

However, in spite of these efforts the promotion of entrepreneurship is very slow in India, particularly in backward areas. Several studies have revealed that the existing constraints are numerous and the efforts could remove them very marginally. For example, study by Planning Commission states, "There have been problems of entrepreneurial augmentation partly due to lack of industrial, cultural and inadequate local activities coupled with serious gaps in infrastructure. "The study further states, "The initiative to establish industrial units usually came from the individuals themselves rather than through any systematic identification and selection of prospective entrepreneurs[k]".

This author, during his research study "Industrial Development in Backward Regions in India[l]", also came across many first generation entrepreneurs who came with lot of hopes and aspirations but turned into a frustrated lot due to several environmental factors and lack of support base. An attempt has, therefore, been made in this study to examine :

(a) Socio-economic environment and its impact on entrepreneurial growth in India.
(b) Impact of institutional initiatives on entrepreneurial augmentation, particularly in backward areas.
(c) Efficacy of incentives and other promotional measures in inducing potential entrepreneurs.
(d) Nature of emerging First Generation Entrepreneurial Class.
(e) Factors responsible for entrepreneurial augmentation.

This study has been based on the extensive field study conducted in two Indian states, namely Maharashtra and Uttar Pradesh, while Maharashtra is one of the leading states, Uttar Pradesh, on the other hand, is one of the less developed states in India. Data has been collected through a specially designed structured questionnaire and personal interviews with the entrepreneurs located in the backward and non-backward districts.

---

k. 'Evaluation Report on Concessional Finance and other incentives in Industrially backward areas' by Programme Evaluation Organisation, Planning Commission, Govt. of India, New Delhi (Nov. 1981) p. 51.
l. Sadhak H: "Industrial Development in Backward Regions in India" Chug Publishers, Allahabad, 1986.

This painstaking study covering the practical experience of several first generation entrepreneurs has thrown light on the shortcomings of the present entrepreneurial development programme, which ought to be removed for healthy growth of entrepreneurs and industrial development. Several policy measures have been suggested to give the programme a new direction and national thrust. An alternative model for entrepreneurship development in rural and backward areas has been suggested. This model takes into account the various socio-economic and cultural mis-matches and emphasised upon promoting an environment conducive to entrepreneurial growth. This model has rural essence and externalities and is a challenge to the ongoing Western Prototype EDP in India.

ACKNOWLEDGEMENT

The present day research work, collection of valuable informations, analysis and final conclusions – all need active support and selfless service from elders and youngers alike. I wish I could mention all their names as a token of my gratitude! I shall be failing in my moral duties, if some names of my guides and friends are not remembered by me.

I am specially indebted to my research guide Dr. K.M. Gavaskar (Poona), who has not only enlightened me many of the crucial issues of this work but also acted as a source of inspiration and support base, particularly at the time of vulnerability.

I am also indebted to Mr. K. Roy, eminent management consultant and an EDP expert with SISI (Kanpur) for this valuable comments on the many issues of the work.

Few among, others who have always extended their support during my study are, Mr. C. Seal (DGM, IDBI), Dr. P. Asthana (GM, IDBI), *Mr R.C. Chadha (ZMLIC)*, Mr. R.L. Srivastave (DGM, IFCI), Dr. N.P. Singh (Director, IED, Lucknow), Dr. S.K. Srivastava, Mr. S.D.D. Tripathi, Mr. A.K. Bose (IIT Kanpur), Dr. A.K. Sarkar, Mr. S.N. Shukla, Mr. K.B. Saxena (Kanpur). I recorded my sincere thanks for their assistance and cooperation.

I have also received lot of encouragement and necessary support from Dr. Dimitar Mircev, (Director, Institute of Self Management, Yugoslavia) *Mr. Karl Fredrickssan (TNA, Sweeden)* Dr. S.N. Srivastava (Economist, Kanpur), Sri S.Mitra (G.M., Lal Imli), Sri Probal Roy (Chairman, TWDC, N. Delhi), Dr. R.P. Sarkar (Director General, Meteorology, N. Delhi), *Mr. C.P. Gupta,* Regional Director, N.P.C. (Kanpur), Dr. M. Sarkar (Jt. Secretary, UGC Delhi), Prof. Y.S. Mahajan, M.P. (Chairman, Centre for Public Sector Studies & Vice Chairman, Parliamentary Forum on Public Sector). My sincere thanks are due to them.

There are several organisations which have always stood by me and helped with the necessary information and publications. Few of them are ICICI (Bombay), IDBI (Bombay), EDI (Lucknow), GIIC (Ahmedabad) SICOM & MIDC (Bombay), UPICON (Kanpur).

UPSIDC (Kanpur) etc. I acknowledge my thanks for their whole hearted cooperation.

I would like to express my thanks to the eminent economist *Dr. R.R. Barthwal, Prof. of Economics, IIT, Kanpur*, who inspite of his very busy schedule has gone through the work and also written the Forward. I shall always remain indebted to him for his constant guidance and inspiration.

Finally, I shall be feeling guilty if I do not mention the tremendous forebearance of my wife, Manjushri, and my son, Partha Pratim, during the course of this study. Manjushri, in addition to shouldering the family responsibilities, while I was struggling with study after normal office hours, has also helped me in preparing the manuscript. However, they can now enjoy the success with me.

H. Sadhak

FORWARD

The economic development of a country to a large extent depends on effective entrepreneurship. It is a function of seeing investment and production opportunities, organizing an enterprise and initiating a process of innovation in order to achieve higher economic-efficiency and thus accelerating the pace of development. In India, inspite of much emphasis on planning during the Post-Independence period, the process of development could not bring desired changes in the socio-economic scene of the country particularly in rural and backward areas. The industrial development which is taken as a major instrument of economic development and change remained more or less sluggish during this period. There might be several factors responsible for this but the single most important factor probably was the absence of effective entrepreneurship. This is, of course, an empirical issue which requires intensive investigations. Dr. Sadhak made an effort in this direction in this valuable book on the subject.

Dr. Sadhak has examined the process of entrepreneurial development and industrial change in the rural and backward areas keeping in view the various measures initiated by the Government and development institutions for them. The efficacy of the policy and programmes for entrepreneurial development has been examined by the author in the light of the data collected through intensive field study. Dr. Sadhak has advocated for rationalization of various efforts and effective restructuring of the current programmes. He has presented a structural planning model which emphasized upon involvement participation and attitudional changes at various levels through development of industrial culture and entrepreneurial environment.

This book, in my view, is an important contribution in the field of rural and backward area development. It will be very useful to the planners, policy makers, bankers, researchers, teachers and students. and the general public interested in the study of economic development. Dr. Sadhak deserves a congratulation for this work.

(R.R. Barthwal)
Professor of Economics

1

ROLE OF ENTREPRENEURS IN INDUSTRIAL DEVELOPMENT

Introduction

Industrialization has become the undisputed path of world wide economic development in modern times. It (Industrialization) has been accepted as an instrument to bring a radical transformation in socio-economic life of traditionally agriculture-based underdeveloped countries. Colman and Nixon said "Industrialization of a basically agricultural-primary export oriented economy was seen as the means by which the chains of dependence forced during the colonial period could be broken matching the newly acquired political independence with economic independence."[1]

It has also been hoped that industrialization would bring social transformation through social equality in higher levels of employment, more equitable distribution of income and well balanced regional development.[2]

Since the industrialization have better potentiality (than agriculture) to bring technological revolution through innovation to attain higher rate of return on social investment, to generate dynamism in social and political life, the newly freed underdeveloped countries have gone for quick industrial development.

The rate of industrial development in any country is determined by social, economic and political conditions. But in developing countries a variety of factors like—lack of industrial environment, lack of incentives for private initiatives, lack of technical knowledge, lack of resources, absence of domestic market, lack of efficient entrepreneurs etc. deter the sustained rate of growth in Industrial Sector.

In fact, the inadequate supply of efficient and motivated entrepreneurs in developing countries is the most important deterrent to faster industrial development in these countries. The slow growth of industries in the developing countries, as the United Nations Economic Commission for Latin America has noted is due "to the absence of properly qualified entrepreneurial class prepared to take initiatives and assume risks and to an inadequate economic policy on the part of Government.[3]

Since entrepreneurs' competence is an important determining factor of rate of growth of industries, absence of competent and motivated entrepreneurial class very often sets the limits to industrial growth and thereby economic development and social change of such countries.

Now the question arises: Who is an entrepreneur? What are the characteristics of an entrepreneur? How the supply of competent entrepreneurs can be augmented in a developing country?

The answers to the above questions are not very simple, because of variety of opinions among economists and social scientists about the character and role of entrepreneurs in economic development. Much of the confusion arises due to variety of definitions at different stages of development. However, attempt has been made by Mark Casson[4] to put the whole approach into two categories, namely 'Functional Approach' and 'Indicative Approach'. While the functional approach specifies some functions of entrepreneurs, the indicative approach provides some description of an entrepreneur by which we can identify him. Once identification problem is solved, we are confronted with the problem of short supply of such entrepreneur, particularly in a developing country. However, there is no unanimous prescription as to how the supply of entrepreneurs can be increased in a country. Basically there are two schools of thought—'Psychologists' & 'Sociologists'— on promoting entrepreneurship in a country.

According to Peter Kilby "the theories of entrepreneurial supply are constructed from either psychological or sociological elements."[5] These theories try to identify social and psychological factors governing the appearance of the entrepreneurs and further, the role of social groups and social mechanism by which individuals are recruited into business occupations. However, the theoreticians are not unanimous about the role and functions of entrepreneurs. While some have defined entrepreneurs as 'the co-ordinator and risk bearer' others have defined him as 'technical innovator' and 'adopter'. Even the motives behind entrepreneurship are different. While economists have thought the 'profit' as the primary motive, the psychologists thought that 'achievement motivation' is the supreme in the mind of entrepreneurs. Therefore, there is no single method to identify the role, function and characteristics of entrepreneurs. We shall therefore, examine some of the leading theories on entrepreneurship to find out the major traits of entrepreneurs and factors determining the supply of competent entrepreneurs in a society.

Some Leading Theories on Entrepreneurship

Richard Cantillon[6]

Richard Cantillon, who wrote in the early 18th century, first coined the term 'Entrepreneurs' to identify those who buy services and sell it. According to Cantillon, the inhabitants of a country except princes and landlords are divided into two categories, viz. 'Entrepreneurs' and 'hired people'. In Cantillon's framework an entrepreneur buys services at certain prices for selling his products at uncertain prices thus bearing a great risk. According to Cantillon, farmers and merchants are also entrepreneurs.

J.B. Say[7]

The Function of entrepreneurs has broadly been described at the first time by Jean Baptiste Say who maintained that the entrepreneurs bring together the factors of production and bear the risk. The success of entrepreneurs depend on their judgement of future demand, estimation of appropriate timings and input. His ability to calculate production cost, selling prices and administrative capabilities make him different from other.

C. Leon Walras[8]

Leon Walras, first developed the notion of general equilibrium and thought that the entrepreneurs are the co-ordinators of other factors of production, i.e. land, labour and capital. Entrepreneur, in his scheme, is a profit maximiser and his endeavour is to move production to equilibrium. The entrepreneur would expand output when selling price is more than the production cost, i.e. the price paid to the owner of the productive services. Output is contracted when selling price falls short of the price of the productive services. Leon Walras, thus, made the entrepreneur a Central Figure of production in economics.

Joseph Schumpeter[9]

The most celebrated theory on entrepreneurship was propounded by the Harvard University Professor Joseph Schumpeter, who brought the conceptual change in the definition and function of entrepreneurs. Entrepreneur, according to Schumpeter is a 'Key functionary of economic development'. Development in Schumpeter's concept is only such changes in economic life which are not forced upon it from outside but originate by its own initiative from within. Schumpeter says that development is a distinct phenomenon entirely foreign to what may be observed in the circular flow or in the tendency towards equilibrium. It is spontaneous and discontinuous change in the channels of the flow, which forever alters and displaces the equilibrium state previously existing. In such a process of development the entrepreneur who carry out 'innovation' or 'new combinations' is the prime mover of economic development. Schumpeter's entrepreneur is therefore an innovator. Schumpeter has referred to five types of innovations :

1. The introduction of a new good or a new quality of a good.
2. The introduction of a new method of production.
3. The opening of a new market.
4. The conquest of new source of supply of raw materials.
5. The carrying out of the new organisation of any industry.

Anyone who carry out the above functions is called 'entrepreneur' in Schumpeter's scheme of things. The entrepreneur may be independent businessman or dependent employee like managers, members of board of Directors, etc. Schumpeter assumed that the essential function of entrepreneurs are always mixed up with other kinds of activities but the carrying out of new combinations is a special function.

Schumpeter's model begins with a circular flow similar to a stationary economy. An entrepreneur in this system is motivated by money profit who introduces innovation. The entrepreneur who innovates has no data to fall back upon and has to depend upon his guess and initiatives. Schumpeter believes that the credit for innovation will be advanced by capitalist for which the capitalist earns interest and the entrepreneur earns profit—by utilising that credit. The function of credit is to force the economic system into new channels.

Schumpeter tried to trace out the motive of entrepreneur behind innovation, which according to him are:

1. There is the dream and will to found a private kingdom—a nearest approach to medieval lordship possible to a modern man.
2. There is the will to conquer—the impulse to fight to other.
3. There is the joy of creating or getting things done—

Schumpeter believes that such type of people who carry out innovations are much less in number and that makes them special type.

Schumpeter was the first economist to develop a comprehensive theory of entrepreneurship and analysed the role of entrepreneurs in economic development through circular flow, nevertheless it suffers from many inbuilt, shortcomings. E.W.Nafziger[10] has pointed out that Schumpeter's theory is purported to have validity only in capitalist economies prior to the rise of giant corporations. This theory has only limited applicability in less developed country. Further, this theory can not be tested empirically because the persons performing entrepreneurial functions can not be identified. Schumpeter has also not clearly stated about the supply of entrepreneurs. Peter Kilby[11] says that the great bulk of Schumpeter's analysis is concerned not with supply of entrepreneurship but with the reactions of the economic system. However, in spite of shortcomings, it should be admitted that Schumpeter has put the entrepreneur theory on sound footing by making the entrepreneur a key functionary of economic development.

Frank Knight[12]

According to Frank Knight the entrepreneur is the recipient of 'pure profit' which is a residual left over after payment of all categories of contractual costs. In Knight's model, the primary function of entrepreneur is to bear non-insurable risk and uncertainties for which he receives the reward (or profit).

There are two types of risk: Insurable and non-insurable. The former can be insured while the later is not. Insurable risk can be calculated statistically and precautionary measures can be taken, while the non-insurable risk cannot be calculated and therefore no precautionary measures can be taken. Entrepreneur in such an uncertain situation has to play the role of a special functionary and the success or failure depends on the foresight and judgement of the entrepreneur.

In Knight's view, the level of profit and the supply of entrepreneurs depend on the elasticity of supply of self confident people.

The entrepreneur in Knight's model bears the risk— a function which is performed by capitalist in Schumpeterian model. However, Knight is more explicit about the profit than Schumpeter.

Leibenstein[13]

Harvey Leibenstein departs from the neo-classical theorists and maintained that the entrepreneurs have only a trivial role to play in a economic model which assumed complete certainty. 'Entrepreneurship' according to Leibenstein is a creative response to 'X-efficiency', which is the degree of inefficiency of the resource use in the firm and the extent to which the firm fails to realise its productive potential. Entrepreneurial opportunity is created due to inefficiency of other people resulting into inefficiency of the organisation that employ them. Entrepreneur in this model is an individual or group of individuals who perform two main functions: Firstly, the entrepreneur acts as a 'input completer' by making available inputs, which improve efficiency of existing production method.

Secondly, the entrepreneur acts as a 'gap filler'. Leibenstein believes that there is no 'one to one correspondence' between inputs and outputs. The entrepreneur has, therefore, to search, discover and evaluate economic opportunities. They have also to arrange for financial capital and have to bear the responsibility of management. These are special qualities rarely available.

The demand for entrepreneurs is determined by the opportunities for 'gap fillers' and 'input completer'. About Leibenstein's theory, Mark Casson says that "in a world where information is costly and has an opportunity cost of time and effort, Leibenstein's individual behave quite rationally. In operational terms, their behaviour seems indistinguishable from rational individuals coping with the constraints imposed by limited information.

David McClelland[14]

David McClelland has developed a psychological theory of entrepreneurial supply centering around the concept of n-achievement (the need for achievement) in his book 'The Achieving

Society'. McClelland believes that the need for achievement is largely for economic development. A society with a generally high level of n-achievement will produce more energetic entrepreneurs, who in turn produce more rapid economic growth.

McClelland used the term entrepreneur not in the sense of capitalist which connotes ownership. Entrepreneur is simply someone who exercises control over production that is not just for personal consumption. The entrepreneurs are different individuals with high n-achievement.

McClelland has noted three major ingredients of the behaviour of an entrepreneur. They are:

1. Desire to take personal responsibility for decision.
2. Preference for decision involving a moderate degree of risk.
3. Interest in concrete knowledge of the results of decision.

McClelland believes that a society with high level of n-achievement will produce more entrepreneurs who in turn would assist more rapid economic development. He prescribed the promotion of an achievement oriented ideology in a country, by inculcating the achievement motivation in child rearing system.

There has been conceptual differences among theoreticians about the basic thesis of McClelland. S.P. Schatz[15] has maintained that the data selected by McClelland to test the theory does not support his hypothesis. Some authors have questioned about the forces to increase the frequency of n-achievement of the society. However, in spite of the doubt about the data and reservation about McClelland's process of economic development, the theory of n-achievement has further developed the psychological base of entrepreneurial theory and given a new direction to the entrepreneurship development, particularly in a developing economies.

Everett Hagen[16]

Hagen in his theory of social change characterised an entrepreneur as a creative personality with high need for achievement, order and autonomy and appears as a problem solver in the process of social transition.

In Hagen's schemes, development do not depend upon the economic factors like spread of market, capital accumulation, perception of profit etc. 'Development' as Hagen viewed is a process of technological change and brought about by a high degree of creativity in few individuals and a moderately high level in a large number. This creativity is nothing but problem solving ability and a tendency to use it. These creative energies are channelled into innovation of technology and physical world rather than in act of war philosophy or politics.

Hagen discussed about the personality complex. To him there are two types of personality—Creative and Uncreative. The Creative personality characterised by high need (for) achievement, high need autonomy, high need order and a sense of the phenomena about one which is conceptually comprehensible. 'Uncreative personality', which is also called 'Authoritarian personality'—characterised by low need achievement and high need dependence, high need submission and dominance and a sense of the world as consisting of arbitrary forces. This authoritarian personality typically exists in traditional society, particularly due to 'Childhood environment and training'.

Hagen assumed that changes in the personality due to status withdrawal of some group or groups of lesser elite transform a traditional state to continuing economic development and once status withdrawal occurs there appears the group of creative individuals alienated from traditions.

F.W. Young[17]

Entrepreneurs in Schumpeter and McClelland's models are identified, through psychological elements. F.W. Young on the other hand given a macro-sociological interpretation of entrepreneur.

The entrepreneur in Young's model is identified by sociological elements rather than psychological elements. Instead of working at individual, Young thought of Clusters—"ethnic communities, occupational groups or politically oriented factions." Showing certain reactiveness or solidarity. A group will be reactive when it experience low status recognition and denial of access to resources but possess a greater degree of resources. However, all the groups do not develop solidarity but the groups with relatively high differentiation react and some members of these solidarity groups excel at combining resources, labour capital, etc. in new ways and they become the entrepreneurs. These solidarity groups perform the entrepreneurial functions like, recombination of economic factors, higher standard of labour, the search for new resources, technology, markets and a more disciplined management of money and time. Example of solidarity group in India is Marwari and Parsi business community.

From the above discussion it can be observed that the concept of entrepreneur and entrepreneurship have intermingled. The concept of entrepreneur and his function has been seen by different authors from different angles. The major points that arises in the light of above theories can be listed below :

1. Entrepreneur is a co-ordinator of factors of production and he manages production and sales.
2. Entrepreneur is a co-ordinator of factors of production— land–labour and capital. He is a profit maximiser and endeavour to reach to equilibrium.
3. Entrepreneur is an innovator, who innovates new production method, market, source of raw materials, etc. The entrepreneur is motivated by monetary gain i.e. profit.
4. Entrepreneur is a risk bearer who works under uncertain situa-tion and he received reward in terms of pure profit.
5. Entrepreneur is a gap filler and input completer.
6. Entrepreneur exercise controls over production which is not just for personal consumption.
7. The entrepreneur is a creative personality who appears as a problem solver in the process of social transformation.
8. Entrepreneurs are 'Solidarity Group' excel at combining resources.

There are 4 important qualities of a successful entrepreneurs— intelligence, motivation, knowledge and opportunity— which can further be subdivided as under: Capacity to take risk, capacity to work hard, desire for deferred consumption, capacity to take advantage of external situation, inventive ability— initiative, imagination, emulation, sociability, flexibility, informative and technical knowledge.

Some of the above qualities are inherent but most of them are self acquired.

Some of the above theories have also discussed about the supply of entrepreneurs. Three important theories are : psychological theory of Schumpeter and McClelland, and sociological theory of Young and Hagen. In Schumpeter's model the entrepreneur is not a function of social, religious and cultural factor, he is the product of strong will power having desired to innovate and to assist economic development. The entrepreneur in McClelland's model is one who has strong n-achievement and the product of Child Rearing System. Everett Hagen argued that the emergence of a substantial number of entrepreneurs depends on the suppression of a previously prestigious group and the slow change in personality. Frank Young believes that the entrepreneurs are the 'Solidarity Groups' who excel in combining resources and it is sociological rather than psychological factors which influence the supply of entrepreneurs.

State as Entrepreneurs

We have discussed about the character, functions and supply of private entrepreneurship and the assumption is that the entrepreneurship is a psychological phenomena and the entrepreneurial supply is influenced more by psychological factors, though sociological factors exert considerable influence. But, the modern industrial development largely depends on the government initiatives and existing economic rules and environment. Therefore entrepreneurial supply is strongly influenced by government initiatives and actions.

In developing countries, where market forces are very weak, socio-psychological factors exert less influence. A large part of economic activities particularly industrial activities are guided and controlled by state mechanism and therefore, the entrepreneurial development to a great extent depend on the state policy.

Apart from indirect control over entrepreneurship the state also directly takes up entrepreneurial activities in the field of material production and infrastructure development through state sector (Public Sector) enterprises. The necessity of direct entrepreneurial activity of the state arise, as Glery Shirokov[18] points out, because

1. State can overcome the obstacles to the introduction of machines that derive from the developing countries socio-economic situations.
2. The state, through taxes, domestic and external loans and deficit financing has been able to provide the measures of centralisation in accumulation that a transition from traditional to modern production requires.
3. State can ignore the profitability criteria of production and assured the construction of mechanised enterprises that are beyond the capacity of private business.
4. Moreover, the state can ensure the equity and distributive justice better through direct industrial initiatives.

In view of the above the newly independent states have taken a major role in industrial activities particularly in manufacturing field through establishment of state enterprises. Therefore, supply of private entrepreneurs are conditioned not only by the socio-psychological factors but also by the degree of state initiatives and mechanism of state controls. Entrepreneurship development in India—a mixed economy with high degree of state control—have influenced by the policy of state initiatives and public enterprises.

Alternative Concept of Entrepreneurship

An entrepreneur has been defined as a coordinator of factors of production, a profit maximiser, a risk bearer, an innovator, a creative person, an agent of social change, etc. All these classical definitions have attempted to define an entrepreneur keeping in view the functions performed by him. There is no doubt that these functional definitions have almost identified the role of entrepreneur in production system in particular and society in general. However, by accepting the definitions which are closely linked to functional aspects, we shall be ignoring most important characteristics of entrepreneur i.e. inner factors leading him to take up the very risky function of entrepreneurship. These forgotten factors can be taken into account by defining an entrepreneur as a "self actualising person" with a high degree of biological instinct of survival (of the fittest). Self actualising person is a person intending to use his capacity, skill and knowledge in a mature and productive way. This type of persons have a very high degree of survival instinct. The self actualising persons, in order to realise self actualisations, initiate and execute such socially relevant development activities through which they can derive self satisfaction and promote social benefits. These enterprising self actualising people with strong biological instinct venture into various productive activities including manufacturing and turned into entrepreneurs, because entrepreneurship offer them tremendous opportunities for utilisation of productive capacities and skill and pave the way for vertical as well as horizontal mobility.

They can structured their own way to give meaningful expression of their ideas. These self actualising entrepreneurs are idealistic as well as realistic. Idealism, which is the product of the desire for more mature and productive utilisation of skills knowledge and capacity lead these people to try to achieve something more than the immediate and long-run personal gain through their activities. Achieving monetary gains also not the primary consideration of their activities. They want to express themselves through some outstanding social gains. The urge for self actualisation make them more innovative and responsive to social change.

Biological instinct of survival encourage them to fight the odds and enthuse them to act towards goals. They have the capacity and mentality to share the burden and bear the risk. Therefore, the biological instinct of survival of the fittest and desire for self actualisation make the self actualising person to initiate and organise. The self actualisation hypothesis lead them to work for socially beneficial production activities while realism — the product of biological instinct of survival— force them to structured realistic approach for the cause (production).

There is no dearth of these 'self actualising persons with high degree of biological instinct for survival'. However, in a society like India, which is characterized by uneven distribution of wealth, concentration of power, existence of heterogeneous social practices and stigma, these self actualising entrepreneurs most often remain dormant due to adverse socio-economic forces. If the necessary environment conducive to self actualisation can be created through institutional actions, a large number of such people will come up to take entrepreneurship by breaking the social and economic barriers from the each and every locality, caste and community.

In India, such type of self actualising entrepreneurs can be found not only among educated and trained people but also among indigenous workmen like carpenter, cobblers, blacksmith, agriculturist, petty shopkeepers who cherish the desire for self advancement and self actualisation. It is the society, which has to create the necessary environment to augment their entrepreneurial ability.

These self actualising entrepreneurs not necessarily be highly educated or from upper strata of society.

This type of enterprising people can be found in all strata of society. They may be highly educated professionals, managers administrators or petty workmen like cobblers, blacksmiths, carpenters, petty shopkeepers even agriculturists. They cherish the desire to fulfil their goal (self-actualisation) but very often fail due to adverse social and economic environment. Therefore, it is the responsibility of the society to come forward to create necessary environment for these people to act.

The hypothesis, that outlined above lead us to the conclusion that entrepreneurs are not merely made, but they are born like trees. However, the scientifically developed surroundings assist them to grow. A tree may be born anywhere but its growth will be conditioned by the surroundings, i.e. condition of water, air, light, etc. whether a tree will spread out its branches or roots will depend on the above conditions. Similarly, the growth of a self-actualising entrepreneurs will depend on the creation of necessary social and economic environment

REFERENCES

1. D. Colman and P. F. Nixon, 'Economics of Changes in Less Developed Countries' Philip Allan Publisher Ltd., Oxford (1978), p. 180.
2. UNIDO, 'Industrial Development Strategy' reprinted in "Leading Issues in Economic Development" (ed. by Gerald M. Meier), Oxford University Press, NY (1976), p. 659.
3. UNIDO, 'Industrialization of Developing Countries: Problems and Prospects', (Monograph-17) United Nations, New York, 1969.
4. Mark Casson, 'The Entrepreneur—An Economic Theory', Martin Robertson, Oxford, 1982, p. 22.
5. Peter Kilby (ed.), 'Entrepreneurship and Economic Development', The Free Press, New York, 1971, p. 6.
6. Richard Cantillon, 'Essai Surla Nature Commerce en General', (Translated by Henry Higgs), Frank Cass and Co., London, 1959.
7. J.B. Say, 'A Treatise on Political Economy', Wells & Lilly, Boston.
8. Leon Walras, 'Elements of Pure Economics', George Allen & Unwin, 1954.
9. J.A. Schumpeter, 'The Theory of Economic Development', Harvard University Press Cambridge, Mass, 1934, p. 64.
10. E.W. Nafziger, 'Class, Caste and Entrepreneurship,' East West Centre, University Press of Hawaii, Honolulu, 1978, p. 17.
11. Peter Kilby, 'Entrepreneurship and Economic Development' (ed. Peter Kilby), The Free Press, New York, 1971.
12. F.H. Knight, 'Risk, Uncertainty and Profit' (ed. G.J. Stigler), University of Chicago Press, Chicago, 1971.
13. Harvey Leibenstein, 'General Ex-efficiency, Theory and Economic Development', Oxford University Press, New York, 1978.
14. David McClelland, 'The Achievement Motive in Economic Growth, in Entrepreneurship and Economic Development' (ed. Peter Kilby), The Free Press, New York, 1971.
15. S.P. Schatz, 'n-achievement and Economic Growth: A Critical Appraisal' in 'Entrepreneurship and Economic Development' (ed. Peter Kilby), The Free Press, New York, 1971.

16. E.E. Hagen, 'On the Theory of Social Changes', Homewood, Illinois, Dorsey Press, 1962.
17. F.W. Young, 'A Macro Sociological Interpretation of Entrepreneurship in Entrepreneurship and Economic Development' (ed. by Peter Kilby), The Free Press, N.Y.
18. Glery Shirokov, 'The Industrial Revolution in the East', Progress Publishers, Moscow (1981), p. 92.

2

CHANGING INDUSTRIAL ENVIRONMENT IN INDIA

Industrial Environment in Pre-independent Period

India is a late starter in the field of industrialisation and development planning. The impact of industrial revolution, which brought a major structural change in the Western Society was not felt in India because of its particular relation with British. India was an integral part of metropolis colony of British Imperialism and was under the perpetual exploitation system which blocked the development of any growth oriented activities. According to Shirokov, the low state of development in such colonial countries was due to a combined influence of exogenous and endogenous factors. Shirokov says, "on the one hand the introduction of the elements of capitalist relation and the involvement of colonies into the international division of labour served to disorganize lower structure and on the other hand wide reliance on non-economic methods of compulsion as one of the basic forms of exploitation and wide conservation of precapitalist and transitional forms of socio-economic relations."[1] India as a part of British Colonial system, suffered due to external and internal adverse factors and could make very little progress.

Indian economy before the arrival of British was in the nature of self sufficient rural economy consisting of self-reliant villages and towns of administrative importance. Though agriculture and other primary economic activities were the major source of livelihood, there was a well organised and well developed rural industry sector based on handicraft, stone carving, marble work etc.

Towns were the centres of craft production and served as the nodal points of trade and business. A.I. Medovoy[2] has observed that the growth of such towns increased the sphere of action of commodity money relations, involved the craftsmen and peasants from nearby villages into commodity exchangers, fostered the formation of local market and then closer economic ties between the various parts of the country. Towns like Dacca, Patna, etc. were such big trading centres. The craft towns and ports had also served as links between craftsmen (Indian) and foreign merchants. Prosperous foreign trade was also based on craft production. But the establish of British Colonial rule in India served a severe blow to the growth of Indian trade and industry, East India Company, which established itself after the battle of Plassey in 1757, used India as a source of cheap raw material and other riches. Industrial revolution in Britain created necessity for expansion of market for British goods and the British started using India as a dumping ground for its goods. Medovoy has stated that the policy of 'trade plunder' was augmented by the export of cheap industrial goods from Britain, which had a truly catastrophic effect on the Indian Economy.

Indian crafts not only lost the foreign market but also lost Indian market due to arrival of cheap British goods. However, there was no effort on the part of British Colonialist to increase manufactured production in India. India, therefore, turned into a supplier of cheap raw materials to imperial Britain and a market for its product.

In the middle of 19th century the colonial exploitation took the new form through British Investment. The bulk of British investment was out of money plundered in India. But, the profit was exported to the home country. In fact, there was no real investment by Britishers in India.

However, there was a wind of change in Indian industrial scene due to construction of Railways in 1840. Though the Railways was constructed by the colonial rulers to keep their factories supplied with raw materials, it helped the establishment of factory system in India. Coal mining was started in Bengal and Bihar in 1870's by Britishers. The first Indian Textiles Mill started production in 1854, and after 1870, Cotton Mills expanded rapidly. The first jute mill was established in 1854, while cotton mills were localised in western India particularly in Bombay and Ahmedabad, jute industry was localised in east India particularly around Calcutta. By 1911, India had 700 factories mainly in jute and textiles group (completely depending on imported equipments).

Vast scope of expansion opened before Indian industry on the eve of World War I due to increased war demand and reduction of import of British goods. During the war, jute, coal, textiles and other industries grew rapidly. Steel and cement industries also established in India during the war. However, in spite of industrial growth during the war, no significant structural change took place in industrial sector due to the British policy. British tariffs, duties, taxes etc. were used to improve the competitiveness of British goods.

One of the important feature of post war (World War I) industrial development was the growth of Indian Managing agency system on the line of East India Company. The biggest managing agencies were set up by Tatas, Birlas, Dalmias, Singhanias etc. They were not only engaged in commerce and industries but also assumed responsibilities for setting up stock companies in various fields. Diversified industrial production was initiated by these managing agents particularly Tatas. Tata controlled enterprises in metallurgy, locomotives, textiles, power, chemical, cements and many other fields. However, before the independence, industrial development primarily took place in the small scale and light industries.

There was hardly any development of heavy industries which are the key to industrial development. And this was due to the calculated move of the British Colonialists to keep India as a supplier of raw materials and market for British products. Therefore, not to allow development of any industry which could pose a threat to British interest. The situation changed only after the independence when the Government of India initiated specified measures to establish capital goods and heavy industries in India.

Industrial Environment in Post-independent Period

Colonial Policy of plunder and exploitation delayed industrial development and economic growth in India. Lack of heavy industries, lack of infrastructure, lack of capital, underdevelopment of capital market, restrictions on entrepreneurial growth etc. created hurdle for industrialisation. The task of Government in independent India was, therefore, to restructuring the multi-form Indian economy to generate momentum of growth through faster industrial development. The strategy of industrial development in India has been clearly reflected in its industrial policy, first announced in 1948. Industrial Policy Resolution (1948)[3] defined the Government's tasks in industry and raising the standard of living of people. The resolution has stated that the Government must play a progressive role in the development of industries but the ability to achieve the main objectives should determine the immediate extent of state responsibility.

With the 1948 Resolution on industrial policy, a new era of development had started in India. Greater role, responsibility and control have been assigned to the state. India launched economic planning in 1951, accepted the mixed economic model of growth aimed at coexistence and growth of private and public sector industries, declared a set of policy measures for growth of heavy industries, infrastructures and established a number of financial institutions to speed up the tempo of growth.

The industrial policy resolution of 1956 stressed upon the need to accelerate the development of heavy industries, machine making industries, to expand public sector and to build up a large and growing cooperative sector. The document also stated that all the industries of basic and strategic importance or in the nature of public utility services should be in the Public Sector. In fact the strategic position of public sector in Indian economy was established through 1956 resolution. The spirit of 1956 resolution also determined the objectives of Second Five Year Plan (1956-61) and according to Dr. Gadgil[4] the basic strategy of Indian planning was spelt out at this stage.

Economic environment in post-independent India undergone a significant change with the acceptance of mixed economic system and launching of Five Year Plan in 1951. Economic activities came under greater control and more patronage of the Government with a view to achieve faster growth and balanced development of Indian economy.

The First Five Year Plan was launched in India with the main objective of reconstruction of post–war and post-independent economy through coordination and nationalisation of economic programmes.

Objectives of the Second Five Year Plan were:
(a) to establish heavy and basic industries so as to be, in due course, self-reliant for continuous industrial development and to depend on improved small industry for increased supply of consumer goods.
(b) to provide large infrastructure of communication system, generation and distribution of power, extension of education at all levels.
(c) to make additional provision of irrigation facilities.

The major thrust of the Second Plan was to build a strong and viable heavy industry sector to give a fillip to the further industrial development for faster growth of Indian economy.

The prime position of public sector in Indian economy was

further reflected in the objectives of Fifth Five Year Plan. The approach paper[5] stated that the state will have to take direct responsibility for future development of industries over a wide field in order to promote the cardinal objectives of social justice, self-reliance and satisfaction of basic minimum needs.

The public sector has been assigned prime position in Indian economy, but not at the cost of private sector. The role of private sector has been given due importance and all the necessary inducements and assistance are provided for its growth. Industrial Policy Resolution 1956 states "The Government of India, however, recognise that it would, in general, be desirable to allow such undertakings to develop with as much freedom as possible, consistent with target and objectives of the national plan. Where there exists both the privately and publicly owned units, it would continue to be the policy of state to give fair and non-discriminatory treatment to both of them".[6] In India, pursuance with the Government policy, private sector is playing a very vital role to promote industrialisation. The position of private sector has further been strengthened due to Government policy of liberalisation (followed in 1980's) which created liberal growth of private business in India.

Post-independent period also marked by the concerted efforts to strengthen the position of small scale industries. Industrial Policy Resolution 1948 stated that the cottage and small scale industries have a very important role in national economy, offering as they do, scope for individual, village or cooperative enterprises and means for the rehabilitation of displaced persons.[7] These industries are particularly suited for the better utilisation of local resources and for the achievement of local self-sufficiency in respect of certain consumer goods. The importance of healthy development of small scale industries was thus recognised right from the beginning of industrial development movement in India.

The importance of small-scale industries in India was further acknowledged in the statement of Industrial Policy 1977 which stated "the main thrust of the new industrial policy will be on effective promotion of cottage and small industries widely dispersed in rural areas and small towns".[8] The industrial policy statement of July 23, 1980[9] further stated that the Government is determined to promote such form of industrialisation in the country as can generate economic viability in the villages. To develop such a viable small industry sector several policy measures have been announced to protect them from the competition of large industries, to introduce innovation and technical change for better quality and productivity, to arrange cheaper capital, raw materials, to render assistance for marking and consultancy etc.

Other significant development in the industrial sector during the post-independent period are:

Attempt to promote industries in less developed and backward areas, establishment of several specialised financial institutions, like IDBI, IFCI, ICICI, LIC, UTI, GIC, IRBI, Export Import Bank, etc., establishment of several industrial development organisations, establishment of several training and consultancy organisations for the development of entrepreneurship. We shall discuss about some of the above institutions separately.

It can be noted from the foregoing discussions that the industrial environment in India have undergone a radical change during post-independent period. Government of India has made significant attempts to remove the impediments of growth in order to create tempo of faster growth and balanced development.

Industrial sector in India is expected to undergo a radical change for "accelerated rate of growth during the Seventh Plan through reform of management system as well as the generation of pressure for increased domestic competition" as stated in the draft of Seventh Plan. The draft has further stated that "a climate must be created which is more conducive to growth, reduction of cost and improvement in quality. The modernisation of industry and its technological upgradation will call for strong linkages with the existing large infrastructure and science and technology."[10]

The draft of Seventh Plan has stressed upon the increased productivity, capacity utilisation and building up domestic technological capabilities, better project implementation and the pursuit of policies that would cut down cost of production particularly in the industrial sector.

The foregoing discussions indicate that India has come a long way since the policy of plunders and systematic obstruction to development during colonial rule. The era of planned development and state patronage to industries, started since independence. Indian industry has experienced expansion, diversification and growth momentum during this period.

Disparities in Industrial Development and Backward Areas

One of the most serious problems in Indian economy is the existence of inter regional (inter-state and intra-state) disparities in development. Before independence while the entire country was lagging in industrial and other developmental activities, this problem was not much evident. However, after independence, substantial development has taken place in various economic sectors, particularly in the field of industry. While some of the states have made rapid progress in industrial activities, others have witnessed very slow progress. Therefore, disparities in growth of state economies have widened and the problem of intra-state disparities have assumed a serious proposition. Even in the states, the growth of economic activities are not uniform in all parts. Development has taken place in few pockets instead of being spread over the state. Therefore, inter-state disparities have been emerged in developed as well as in backward states. This problem, which in American Terminology, called North-South Problem can better be called centre-periphery problems, because, in India few developed pockets have been surrounded by vast undeveloped rural areas i.e. plenty amidst poverty.

However, since our major concern is the entrepreneurship development in backward regions, we are not going into the deep of the problem. We shall only discuss about the nature of intra-state disparities and the promotional facilities in respect of development of entrepreneurship in backward regions (district/areas).

Disparities in development among the various states in India have been discussed in terms of simple development indicators like per capita income, unemployment, poverty. Since industrial development has been accepted as the primary instrument of growth an indication has been given about the level of infrastructure development, urbanization and industrialisation in various states in India.

Per capita income is the most crucial indicator of the economic development of any state. Average per capita income in India in 1982-83 was Rs. 1891, but only 5 states viz., Gujarat, Haryana, Maharashtra, Punjab and West Bengal were the above national average. Some of the larger states like Bihar, Orissa, U.P., M.P. were much below the national average.

Employment is another important indicator of development. A well developed economy should be able to provide employment opportunities to the growing population. In absence of reliable datas, to indicate the extent of unemployment in various states, we have used the employment exchange data regarding job seekers. As on 31-5-1985, total job seekers with employment exchanges in various states shown in table 2.1. States which have a very high rate of unemployment are West Bengal, Bihar, A.P., Kerala, Maharashtra, U.P., Tamil Nadu. Further, the unemployment problem is more acute in urban areas as indicated in 38th round of NSS data. Accordingly, in 1983 (Jan-June), daily unemployment rate was as 4.79% and 2.52% respectively among male and female rural areas and 5.45% and 1.72% respectively among male and female in urban areas. A very high percentage of rural unemployment was in Kerala (male 13.39% and female 6.56%), in Tamil Nadu (male 12% and female 5.3%), in West Bengal (male 8.80% and female 0.98%) and in Andhra Pradesh (male 5.5% and female 6.28%). A very high percentage of urban unemployment was observed in Kerala (male 12.76% and female 5.29%), Tamil Nadu (male 9.45% and female 3.48%), West Bengal (male 7.5% and female 1.55%).

Therefore, we find that employment opportunities are not uniformly spread over the states. While some of the states could keep the unemployment problem within the reasonable limit others are suffering from unemployment problems. Even some of the developed states suffer from unemployment problem.

Disparities in development has also been exposed through distribution of people below the line of poverty. Table 2.1 indicates that in 1981-82, 48.1% of the people were below the line of poverty. The percentage was higher than national average in Assam (51.1%), Bihar (57.5%), Karnataka (48.3%), M.P. (57.7%), Orissa (66.4%), Tamil Nadu (52.1%), Tripura (59.7%), U.P. (59.1%), and West Bengal (52.5%). The position was little favourable in the states like Punjab, Haryana, Himachal Pradesh, Gujarat, Maharashtra, J & K. If we examine the poverty situation in relation to per capita income, it can be noted that the states with higher per capita income has lower incidence of poverty except Maharashtra and West Bengal where both were high. The position of West Bengal and Maharashtra is different from other developed states because the development in these states have been concentrated in certain pockets, the hinterland being remained backward. Secondly, excessive population pressure due to migration from other states have increased the incidence of poverty.

Changing Industrial Environment in India

Table 2.1 : Income Unemployment & Poverty

S. No.	States/ Union Territories	Per Capita Income 1982-83	Unemployment[d] (in 000)	Poverty Population below Poverty line No. (lakhs)	As Percentage of population
(1)	(2)	(3)	(4)	(5)	(6)
1.	Andhra Pradesh	1536	2218.8	206.8	42.2
2.	Assam[a]	1380	524.9	95.4	51.1
3.	Bihar[a]	995	2650.2	371.3	57.5
4.	Gujarat[a]	2182	652.8	121.3	39.0
5.	Haryana	2798	456.5	29.1	24.8
6.	Himachal Pradesh	1865	279.0	10.9	27.2
7.	Jammu & Kashmir	1630	68.7	18.9	34.1
8.	Karnataka	1559	810.9	162.7	48.3
9.	Kerala[a]	1447	2461.1	115.6	47.0
10	Madhya Pradesh	1311	1186.1	287.3	57.7
11.	Maharashtra	2525	2102.8	275.4	47.7
12.	Manipur[a]	1045	195.7	4.0	29.7
13.	Orissa[a]	1308	603.0	169.3	66.4
14.	Punjab	3484	543.3	23.1	15.1
15.	Rajasthan	1574	560.0	104.9	33.8
16.	Tamil Nadu[a]	1373	1795.6	237.1	52.1
17.	Tripura[c]	1095	95.4	11.5	59.7
18.	U.P.	1439	2089.1	502.0	59.1
19.	West Bengal	19595	4103.5	275.8	52.5
	Union Territories :				
20.	Delhi[a]	3208	502.6	17.6	⎫
21.	Goa, Daman, Diu[a]	2891	46.1	--	⎬ 21.7[e]
22.	Pondicherry[b]	2928	68.1	3046.1	⎭
	All India	1891	24179.5	3046.1	48.1

Notes : (a) Data relates to 1981-82
      (b) Data relates to 1980-81
      (c) Data relates to 1979-80 (—) Nil or Negligible
      (d) Unemployment indicate figures of job seekers with employment exchanges on 31.5.85
      (e) This percentage has been arrived by taking together all the Union Territories.

Source : Basic Statistics of State Economies of India, Commerce Research Bureau, Bombay (Oct. 1986).

The disparities among various states would be more evident if we look into some of the important indicators of industrial development. Two most important industrial indicators are value added by manufacturing and percentage of workers in manufacturing activities. Since industrial development is strongly influenced by the level of infrastructure development, we need to see the level of infrastructure development in various states. Further, the industrial development is closely related to urbanisation. A high degree of urbanisation is an assisting factor for faster industrial growth. Now, let us see the level of development of infrastructure, urbanisation and industrial development (Table 2.2).

The infrastructure index has been constructed by taking into account contribution of power, transport, irrigation, banking, education, health to the state economies. These are the preconditions for industrial development. The rate of development depends on these factors.

The infrastructural development has been very uneven in India. The states like Punjab, Haryana, Tamil Nadu, Kerala, West Bengal, Gujarat and Maharashtra achieved a high degree of infrastructural development. There is a strong positive correlation between infrastructural development and industrialisation. Industry can be located at any particular place having necessary and developed infrastructural facilities. Further, there is a strong positive correlation between urbanisation and industrial development. It is very difficult to say which lead whom, but it can be said that both are very much dependent on each other. The most urbanised states in India are Maharashtra, Tamil Nadu, Gujarat, Karnataka, Punjab, and West Bengal. These states have achieved a high degree of infrastructural as well as industrial development. If the indicator of value added by industry is considered, we can observe from the data in table 2.2 that Maha-rashtra, West Bengal, Tamil Nadu, Gujarat, U.P., Karnataka and A.P. are the top seven states in India. A relatively high percentage of workers are also employed in manufacturing sector in these states.

It is, evident that the states in India having a higher rate of per capita income are usually those which have achieved a higher rate of growth in industry and better development in infrastructure and urbanisation.

Changing Industrial Environment in India 25

Table 2.2 : **Infrastructure Urbanisation and Industrial Development**

Sl. No.	States	Index of infrastructure 1981-82	Urbanisation (Per cent) (1981)	Industrial Development Per cent value added to all India (1980-81)	workers employed in mfg. Industries (1971)
(1)	(2)	(3)	(4)	(5)	(6)
1.	Andhra Pradesh	96(10)	23(8)	4.9	9.0
2.	Assam	95(11)	9(21)	1.0	4.0
3.	Bihar	102(9)	12(18)	4.2	5.1
4.	Gujarat	123(6)	31(3)	9.5	12.0
5.	Haryana	157(2)	22(9)	2.9	10.0
6.	Himachal Pradesh	83(16)	8(22)	0.5	3.9
7.	Jammu & Kashmir	85(13)	19(12)	0.2	6.8
8.	Karnataka	94(12)	29(4)	5.1	10.2
9.	Kerala	135(4)	19(13)	3.3	15.8
10.	Madhya Pradesh	71(19)	20(11)	5.1	6.6
11.	Maharashtra	116(7)	35(1)	25.0	13.1
12.	Manipur	85(14)	26(6)	—	11.0
13.	Meghalaya	66(20)	18(14)	0.1	—
14.	Nagaland	85(15)	16(16)	NA	—
15.	Orissa	83(17)	12(19)	1.7	5.9
16.	Punjab	246(1)	28(5)	3.2	11.3
17.	Rajasthan	75(18)	21(10)	2.8	6.6
18.	Sikkim	66(21)	16(17)	—	—
19.	Tamil Nadu	144(3)	33(2)	10.3	13.3
20.	Tripura	62(22)	11(20)	—	3.5
21.	Uttar Pradesh	114(8)	18(15)	6.3	7.3
22.	West Bengal	131(5)	26(7)	11.5	14.1
23.	Union Territories	—	—	2.4	—
	All India		100	24	100	9.4

Source : 'Basic statistics on State Economies of India; Commerce Research Bureau, Bombay (October, 1986).

The data in Table 2.3 indicate that backward states are generally lagging in industrial development. However, attempts have been made to reduce backwardness and to remove intra-state disparities in development primarily through promotion of industries in relatively less developed or backward states. Though India launched its Planning in 1951, it did not make any particular attempt to tackle the problem of intra-state disparities till the Third Five Year Plan, which emphasised upon the necessity to reduce regional (inter intra-state) disparities and to attain balanced regional development. Special attention has been paid to develop industries in the lagging states. India has followed a wide course of action to attract industries in lagging states. It has mainly relied on incentive measures instead of strong regulatory measures like location control.

Before 1969, the important instruments used to attract industrial investment in backward states/regions were : Licensing policy- aiming at dispersing industries from congested areas and to control industrial location, Public Sector investment in backward states/ regions—to encourage the growth of ancillaries and create a momentum of growth : and establishment of industrial estate—to develop infra-structural facilities for the small and medium industries etc. However, these measures could not bring any significant charge in the inter regional disparities in industrial development.

It was therefore necessary to take some concrete measures to tackle the problem of regional disparities. Planning Commission, therefore, appointed 2 Working Groups.

1. Working Group on Identification of Backward Areas (Chairman Sri B.D. Pandey)[11]
2. Working Group on Fiscal and Financial Incentives for starting industries in backward regions. (Chairman N.N. Wanchoo)[12]

The Pandey Committee on the basis of some selected indicators like, Total/Per capita income, per capita income from Industry and Mining, workers in registered factories, per capita consumption of electricity, length of surface road, Railway mileage etc. identified certain states and districts as backward. On the basis of the principal recommendations, the Government of India in 1971, notified 217 districts as backward districts. On the basis of the recommendation of Wanchoo Committee, the Government declared certain incentives measures like capital investment subsidy and transport subsidy in

Table 2.3 : Area and Population under Industrially Backward Districts

	States/Union Territories		District/ Area under category A,B, & C	P.C. under backward area Total state area	P.C. under backward area Total state population
1.	Andhra Pradesh	(23)	19	73	57
2.	Assam	(16)	10	160	100
3.	Bihar	(37)	17	52	54
4.	Gujarat	(19)	11	69	49
5.	Haryana	(12)	7	39	33
6.	Himachal Pradesh	(12)	12	100	100
7.	Jammu & Kashmir	(14)	14	100	100
8.	Karnataka	(19)	11	66	61
9.	Kerala	(13)	7	59	55
10.	Madhya Pradesh	(45)	41	80	71
11.	Maharashtra	(30)	13	54	39
12.	Manipur	(6)	6	100	100
13.	Meghalaya	(5)	5	100	100
14.	Nagaland	(7)	7	100	100
15.	Orissa	(13)	8	60	48
16.	Punjab	(12)	5	50	40
17.	Rajasthan	(27)	16	62	54
18.	Sikkim	(4)	4	100	100
19.	Tamil Nadu	(17)	12	65	59
20.	Tripura	(3)	3	100	100
21.	Uttar Pradesh	(57)	41	70	63
22.	West Bengal	(17)	13	82	69
	Union Territories				
1.	Andaman Nicobar	(2)	2	100	100
2.	Arunachal Pradesh	(9)	9	100	100
3.	Dadra Nagar Haveli	(1)	1	100	100
4.	Goa Daman & Diu	(3)	1	100	100
5.	Lakshadweep	(1)	1	100	100
6.	Mizoram	(3)	2	81	87
7.	Pondicherry	(4)	1	100	100
	All India		299	72	60

Sources : (1) Ministry of Industry and Company Affairs, Department of Industrial Development Report, 1984-85.
(2) I.D.B.I. Brocher on Concessional Finance, 1984.

1971 and Income Tax concessions in 1974 for industries in backward regions. These measures i.e. identification of backward regions for intensive development efforts have been partially successful in inducing industrial investment in the backward districts. But, in the process, industrial investment in the backward regions got concentrated. Particularly in backward districts of developed states and the disparities have been widened further. Government of India, therefore, appointed the National Committee on the Development of Backward areas under the Chairmanship of Sri B. Srinivasan which submitted its report in 1981.[13] The committee recommended the identification of backward areas on the basis of fundamental factors which inhibit development. The problems of industrial development in those areas should be considered in terms of structural factors. The committee suggested that the backwardness should be determined on the basis of fundamental backward areas, Tribal Areas, Hill Areas, Drought Prone Areas, Hot & Cold Water Areas, Chronically Flood Affected Areas and Coastal Areas affected by salinity. The committee also suggested the 'block' as an unit to administer the incentives.

The committee has also noted that the central investment subsidy and concessional finance, concentrated to a small No. of districts mostly in West or South. Several other studies have revealed the concentration of concessional finance and investment subsidy in backward districts/areas of relatively developed states. Incentives also encouraged concentration of industries in some pockets of backward districts which have further widened inter-state disparities. It was, therefore, suggested in many studies (including one by this author) to redefine the backward districts on the basis of level of development and to introduce graded scheme of incentives in order to make backward districts/areas more attractive to industries. The Government of India announced the fresh classification of backward districts/areas.[14] Accordingly, backward districts, on the basis of level of development, were classified into 3 categories, viz, 'A', 'B' & 'C'. In 1986, the Govt. of India notified 299 districts as backward of which 131 were 'A' category districts, including 90 'No Industry District' (which have no medium and large scale industrial unit). There were 55 'B' category districts and 113 'C' category districts.

According to 1986 classification 'A' category districts comprises of no industry districts plus special regions. 'B' Category districts comprises of districts which were eligible for central subsidy prior to April '83 minus districts included in 'A' category as above.

'C' Category districts comprises of 246 concessional finance districts minus the districts included in 'A' & 'B' (A list of the districts under 'A', 'B' and 'C' category is given in Appendix-1). The No. of backward districts have increased to 301 and at present, the distribution of backward districts/areas are as following:—

Category 'A'— There are 134 districts comprising of 'No Industry and special region districts.
Category 'B'— There are 54 districts.
Category 'C'— There are 113 districts.

The Central Government has also declared the new scheme of subsidies for the industrial set up in backward districts/areas.

The rate of central subsidy for the 3 categories of districts mentioned above are as under:

Category 'A'— 25% of fixed capital investment subject to a maximum of Rs. 25 lakhs.
Category 'B'— 15% of fixed capital investment subject to a maximum of Rs. 15 lakhs.
Category 'C'— 10% of the fixed capital investment subject to a maximum of Rs. 10 lakhs.

The All India Financial Institutions have also reviewed the scheme of concessional finance and other incentives for setting up in the backward districts particularly in NO INDUSTRY DISTRICTS. Accordingly, the new projects are eligible for concessional rupee finance on aggregate basis from the financial institutions as under:-

Districts/Areas	Loan Assistance (Rs. Crores)	Underwriting Assistance (Rs. Crores)
Category 'A' (NIDS)	5.00	2.50
Category 'B'	3.00	1.50
Category 'C'	2.00	1.00

Source: IFCI Annual Report, 1986-87.

I. The concessional portion of the loan assistance carried

interest @ 12.5% p.a. as against the normal rate of 14% p.a. The rate of underwriting commission is reduced by 50% (on the concessional part of underwriting assistance).

II. The norm of Promoters contribution in 'A' & 'B' category districts has been reduced by 15% of total cost of projects. The same has been reduced to 17.5% in the category 'C' districts.

III. There is also relaxation on commitment charge levied on the undrawn part of rupee loans.

There is the provision for assistance to industries for the development of project specific infrastructure and for the setting up of Nucleus Plants in the central subsidy districts. The rate of central investment subsidy for Nucleus Plans is as following:

'A' Category districts—25% upto a ceiling of Rs. 25 lakhs.
'B' Category districts—20% upto a ceiling of Rs. 20 lakhs.
'C' Category districts—15% upto a ceiling of Rs. 15 lakhs.

Development of Indian Economy Since 1951

We start with the concluding paragraph of an article of eminent international economist Sukhamoy Chakraborty, who says "while our achievements during the last thirty odd years of planning have by no means been insignificant in the area of agricultural production, industrial diversification and technology acquisition, we have not been able to make a major impact on the lives of vast masses of our people. However, consciousness has very much increased. This can be a source of very positive developments."[15] This seems to be the correct assessment of Indian economy since independence and if more specific, since the launching of economic planning. In this section a brief outline on the state of development, particularly in the industrial sector has been given.

National Income

There has been a significant improvement in National Income since the inception of Planning in 1951. Table 2.4 indicates that Gross National Product (GNP) at current prices increased from Rs. 9136 crores in 1950-51 to Rs. 188459 crores in 1984-85. The Net National Product (NNP) at current prices increased from Rs. 8812 crores to Rs. 173207 crores in 1984-85 while the per capita income increased from Rs. 245.5 to Rs. 2343 during the same period. The average annual rate of growth during the above period was 3%.

Changing Industrial Environment in India

Table 2.4 : Gross National Product, Net National Product and Per Capita Net National Product (at factor cost)

	G.N.P. (Rs. Crores)		N.N.P. (Rs. Crores)		Per Capita N.N.P.	
	At Current Prices	At 1970-71 Prices	At Current Prices	At 1970-71 Prices	At Current Prices	At 1970-71 Prices
1950-51	9136	17469	8812	16731	245.5	466.0
1960-61	13999	25424	13263	24250	305.6	558.8
1970-71	36452	36452	33435	34235	632.8	632.8
1980-81	113846	50711	105743	47414	1557.3	698.3
1984-85*	188459	61201	173207	57014	2343.8	771.5

*Quick Estimate.
Source : Economic Survey 1986-87, Government of India.

Though GNP & NNP at 1970-71 prices was Rs. 61201 crores and 57014 crores the same according to new series (1980-81 prices) Rs. 147816 crores and 132367 crores in 1984-85. GNP and NNP were 161298 crores and Rs. 143935 crores in 1986-87. Per Capita Income at 1980-81 prices was 1869.3 during 1986-87 (for detail please see Appendix -ii).

According to new series, GNP growth was 4.9 per cent in 1985-86 and 4.1 per cent in 1986-87. The lower growth rate in 1986-87, according to Economic Survey 1987-88 was due to a decline of nearly 2 per cent of gross value added in the group 'agriculture and allied activities.'

The data in the Table 2.5 shows the annual compound growth rate of GNP, NNP and Per Capita NNP i.e. Per Capita National Income during Five Years Plans in India.

The Gross domestic product at factor cost by industry of origin is shown in Table 2.6 the share of agriculture and allied sector was about 37% to total GDP in 1985-86, whereas the share of industrial sectors was about 22%. In 1985-86, agriculture and allied sector registered only marginal growth over the previous period whereas the growth of service sector was significant. (See Appendix-iii)

Table 2.5 : Annual Growth Rate of Indian Economy

	G.N.P.		N.N.P.		Per Capita N.N.P.	
	At Current Prices	At 1980-81 Prices	At Current Prices	At 1980-81 Prices	At Current Prices	At 1980-81 Prices
First Plan (1951-56)	1.2	3.6	1.0	3.6	(--)0.8	1.7
Second Plan (1956-61)	7.6	4.0	7.4	4.0	5.3	1.9
Third Plan (1961-66)	9.3	2.5	9.2	2.2	6.8	--
Three Annual Plans (1966-69)	11.5	4.1	11.5	4.0	9.1	1.8
Fourth Plan (1969-74)	12.0	3.5	12.0	3.4	9.5	1.1
Fifth Plan (1974-79)	10.2	5.2	10.0	5.2	7.6	2.9
Annual Plan (1979-80)	9.7	(--)4.7	9.2	(--)5.2	6.7	(--)7.3
Sixth Plan (1980-85)*	14.9	5.3	14.6	5.3	11.9	3.0

* These are average annual growth rate for the period 1980-81 (old series) and 1981-82 to 1984-85 (New Series).

Source: Economic Survey, 1987-88.

The rate of growth of domestic capital formation in the economy increased from 23.5% of GDP (at current prices) in 1983-84 to 24.4% in 1985-86, whereas the rate of Gross domestic savings has declined from 22.9% in 1984-85 to 22.8% in 1985-86.

However, there is a trend of faster growth of Indian economy in recent years. Economic Survey 1986-87 states that there is a strong evidence that the Indian economy is now on a new growth path. Aggregate economic growth in the first 2 years of the plan (7th plan) averaged around 5% per year and the momentum of development being sustained by the steady expansion of resource allocated for development expenditure. Dr. V.K.R.V. Rao says that the projected growth rate during the period of 15 years (1985-2000) would be of the order 5 per cent.[16]

Table 2.6 : Gross Domestic Product at Factor Cost by Industry of Origin (at 1970-71 prices)

	Industry Group	1970-71	1975-76	1980-81	1985-86*
1.	Agriculture, Forestry and Logging, Fishing	17802 (8.1)	19934 (13.3)	21015 (12.0)	23998 (1.5)
	Mining and Quarrying				
2.	Manufacturing, Construction	7594 (0.9)	8782 (5.5)	10937 (1.2)	14242 (6.6)
	Electricity Gas & Water	5912 (4.4)	7461 (9.2)	9554 (6.0)	12955 (6.3)
3.	Transport, Communication and Trade	2114 (6.7)	2574 (8.2)	3358 (2.8)	4683 (7.3)
4.	Banking, Insurance real estate and ownership of dwellings and Business				
5.	Public administration defence and other services	3314 (5.0)	4139 (4.9)	5759 (7.9)	9110 (10.1)
6.	Gross domestic product (at Factor Cost)	36736 (5.6)	42890 (9.7)	50623 (7.3)	64988 (5.1)

Note: Figures in brackets indicate percentage change over the previous year.

* Quick estimates

Source: Economic Survey 1986-87, Government of India, Ministry of Finance, 1987.

Agriculture

Indian Planners heavily depended on industrial sector for rapid economic growth of the country and agriculture has been given the secondary place during the process of planned development. In the words of Dr. A. M. Khusro "Planned economies which have decided to bring about a major break through in economic growth have typically adopted the idea of heavy industrialisation to begin with. They gave low priority to consumer goods production but high priority to the production of power, mother machines and machines, which they argued would provide the where withal for agriculture, and at a later stage, of consumer goods production."[17] However, in spite of the absence of sufficient Government attention, Indian agricultural sector has shown a upward trend in agricultural production due to the increasing area under assured irrigation, rising fertiliser consumption, and the higher use of high yielding varieties of seeds along with the Government's policy of assuring remunerative, prices to peasants have pushed up per hectare productivity and raised total production. It has been estimated that during 1960-80 agricultural productivity increased but there is a marked imbalance in regional productivity. While productivity increased by 80% and 57% in Northern and Southern States, the same increased by 27% in the Eastern states, and by 40% in the country as a whole. The economic survey 1986-87 has estimated that the overall foodgrains in 1985-86 was at 150.5 million tonnes. Similar positive trend was also noted in respect of production of non-food crops. The F.A.O. production year book 1981 has stated that by the year 2000, assuming that Indian massive irrigation development plans materialise and irrigations contribution to production increases from the present level of 58 per cent to 87 per cent, even with low level of inputs India's lands will have the capacity to support a population of 1298 million against the assumed population of 1036 million in that year."[18]

Infrastructure

In recent years Indian economy witnessed an improvement in infrastructural sector due to Government's special attention to improve management of economy. Economic Survey 1986-87 states that the current year will be the third consecutive high growth year in the infrastructure sector, recording an increase of around 9-10%. The high growth rate over last three years particularly in the key sectors such as electricity, coal and rail traffic would tend to ease the bottlenecks in the economy and enhance growth process in the other sector of the economy.[19]

The impressive growth of infrastructure industries during the recent years can be noted from the fact that during 1986-87, production of coal was 113.0 Mn tonnes, Electricity generation was 138.6 Billion KWH, Petroleum production was—Crude Oil production 23.0 Mn tonnes and Refinery throughout 33.5 Mn tonnes. Indian Railways also shown improved performance. Revenue earning goods traffic was 199.30 Mn tonnes, and the major parts handled cargo of 88.1 Mn tonnes. Others areas of infrastructure sector also shown improved performance. However, supply of infrastructural inputs in certain areas are still lagging behind the demand. Moreover, the infrastructural facilities are not spatially distributed over the regions.

Industry

India has achieved a remarkable achievement in industrial sector. During the course of planning, it has emerged as leading industrialised country of the world. In spite of several constraints of growth, India has built up a viable self-reliant industrial structure—a solid foundation of basic industries, diversified industrial production and significant growth of industrial output etc. are the clear indication of the dynamism of Indian industry since independence. The significance of industry (and construction) in Indian economy can be seen from the fact that in 1984-85, this sector contributed 21.6% to G.D.P. at factor cost.

Dr. C. Rangarajan states "(Since Independence) aggregate output of industrial sector has increased five fold over a thirty year period giving a compound rate of growth of 6 per cent per annum. The performance looks by even more striking if it judged by the criterion of the range and sophistication of the output manufactured. The cutput of capital goods industries consisting primarily of machinery had a weight of less than of in the index of industrial production in 1956, its weight has increased to almost 15 p.c. in 1970. Basic and capital goods industries taken together account not for 50 p.c. of total value added in industrial production", the share of value added by all engineering industries in the total value added by all industries is 35.4 per cent.[20]

Like industrial output, the No. of industries—Large, medium and small scale—has also increased significantly and industrial sector has emerged as a leading employment sector due to vast expansion and diversification of product lines.

Large and medium scale industries increased from 37100 in 1959 to 95100 in 1985. Employment in these industries increased from 35.7 lakhs in 1959 to 76.8 lakhs in 1985 (Table 2.7). The No. of small scale industries in 1985-86 was 13.53 lakhs which employed 96.0 lakhs employees (Table 2.8). Value of production of small scale sector was Rs. 61,100 crores in 1985-86, SSI sector is also making good contribution to export sector. In 1984-85 total export of SSI sector was Rs. 2579.9 crores.

Table 2.7 : Selected Growth Indicators of Large Scale Industries in India (ASI Data)

Year	Reporting Factories (No. in 00)	Employment in Lakhs Person	Value of output Rs. Crores	Natural Income Generated Rs. Crores
1959	371	35.7	3404	880
1969	602	50.3	12055	2776
1979	951	76.8	52288	10865

Source: Census of manufacturing industries, Annual Survey of industries (Our Source, Basic statistics on Indian Economy, Commerce Research Bureau)

It can therefore be observed from the above that since independence industrial sector in India has registered a significant growth. This growth trend has also been indicated in Economic Survey 1986-87, which states "Industrial growth has accelerated in recent years and buoyant indicators of investment intentions augers well for future industrial expansion. According to the new 1980-81 based index of industrial production, industrial growth accelerated to over 8.5 per cent in 1984-85. For 1985-86 this growth rate was 8.7 per cent. According to the new series, there was significant growth in manufacturing sector which increased from 8.0 per cent in 1984-85 to 9.7 per cent in 1985-86. The survey assumed that the improvement in industrial performance attributed in part to the reduction of procedural impediments to industrial expansion and the growing emphasis on capacity creation, technology, competition and more economic source of production".[21]

Table 2.8: Selected Growth Indicators of Small Scale Industries in India

No. of Units (Reg. & Unreg.) Years	in Lakhs	Employment in Lakhs person	Production (in 1970-71 Prices) Rs. Crores
1978-79	7.34	63.8	8,787
1979-80	8.05	67.0	10,025
1980-81	8.74	61.0	10,906
1981-82	9.62	75.0	11,837
1982-83	10.55	79.0	12,800
1983-84	11.50	84.15	14,040
1984-85	12.42	90.0	5,052
1985-86	13.53	96.0	61,100

Source: (i) Yojana Jan 1-15, 1987.
(ii) Economic Survey 1986-87.

Public Sector

Special mention should be made about the progressive growth and contribution of public sector in Indian economy because of the special role assigned to it. Public sector in India is to direct, motivate and brought a transition in Indian industry and hasten the process of economic development during the process of planning. The public sector has been quite successful in laying a strong foundation for Indian Industry and contributed significantly to employment investment capital formation and economic transition.

In 1986-87, there were 214 running public sector (Central) - enterprises in India. Total turnover of these enterprises was Rs. 69016 crores as against Rs. 47272 crores in 1983-84. Employment in public sector increased from 133.22 lakhs in 1976 to 176.78 lakhs in 1986 as against the increase of 68.44 lakhs to 73.57 lakhs in private sector during the same period. The public sector enterprises contributed Rs. 7536 crores in 1986-87 against Rs. 4654 crores to total Gross Domestic Savings in 1980-81. The contribution of public sector to gross fixed capital formation in India was Rs. 31272 crores in 1986-87. It can be noted from this limited information that the public sector enterprises are playing the dominant role in the

Table 2.9 : Growth Rate of Industrial Production (Percentage)

Sector	Weight		1984-85		1985-86	
	1970 Series	1980-81 Series	1970 Series	1980-81 Series	1970 Series	1980-81 Series
1. General	100.0	100.0	6.8	8.6	6.3	8.7
2. Manufacturing	81.08	77.11	5.7	8.0	6.1	9.7
3. Mining & Quaring	9.69	11.46	8.0	8.8	4.7	4.2
4. Electricity	9.23	11.43	12.0	12.0	8.5	8.5

Source : Economic Survey, 1986-87.

process of development. However, the performance of public sector enterprises in terms of commercial profitability is not that encouraging. But if we consider its contribution to heavy industry building infrastructure development, transferring industrial investment to hitherto neglected backward regions and in the field of essential items, the public sector has definitely done tremendous jobs. Public sector has also created enough opportunities for achievement oriented, creative young people to join as establishment entrepreneurs' in public sector, the field which was otherwise forbidden to people with ordinary background. Public sector enterprises, thus rendered tremendous services for the promotion of entrepreneurship in India.

A Comparative Study of Growth of Relatively Developed and Backward State in India i.e.

Maharashtra[22]

Maharashtra is the fourth largest state, both in terms of area (308000 sq. km.) and population (6.28 crores) in India. It is the most urbanised state in India having 35% of urban population as against 23.7% in India. In terms of literacy it occupies the second position (47%). The state has made rapid progress in industry, infrastructure, agriculture and service sector. Bombay, the business capital of India is located in this state. Even during the British period Bombay gave birth to Indian industry and indigenous entrepreneurs. G.D.P. in Maharashtra in 1982-83 was 6306 crores at 1970-71 prices and the percentage increase between 1970-71 to 1982-83 was 62.7%

Changing Industrial Environment in India

Table 2.10 : Profile of Public Enterprises (1980-81 to 1986-87)

		1980-81	1983-84	1986-87 (Provisional)
1.	No. of running public enterprises (No)	168	201	214
2.	Capital (Rs. Crores)	18207	29851	51931
3.	Turnover (Rs. Crores)	28635	47272	69016
4.	Gross Margin (Rs. Crores)	2401	5771	9894
5.	Depreciation (Rs. Crores)	983	2205	3382
6.	Gross Profit (Rs. Crores)	1418	3565	6512
7.	Interest (Rs. Crores)	1399	2086	3417
8.	Net Profit before Tax (Rs. Crores)	19	1480	3095
9.	Tax (Rs. Crores)	222	1239	1326
10.	Net Profit after Tax (Rs. Crores)	(-) 203	240	1769
11.	Internal resource generated (Rs. Crores)	1225	3695	6097
12.	Gross Profit to Capital employed (Per cent)	7.8	11.9	12.5

Source : Economic Survey, 1987-88.

as against the Indian average of 49.3%. Maharashtra contributed Rs. 6306 crores, i.e. 12.36% which was highest in India in 1982-83. In terms of per capita income Maharashtra occupied third position in India. The per capita income of the state was Rs. 2525 as against average per capita income of Rs. 1819 in India in 1982-83 at current prices. In 1960-61 the primary sector accounted for 38% of S.D.P. and that of service sector was 34%. But, in 1979-80 the share of primary sector declined and the share of manufacturing and service sector.

Agriculture

In the field of agriculture the state could not make as much progress as in the field of industry and infrastructure. Yet the state could make better progress than many other states in irrigation and food production. Maharashtra has extensive area under cultivation and ranked second in terms of net area sown in 1977-78. Maharashtra has got 20,386 thousand hectares agricultural area (up to 1984-85), irrigation potential was created for 3697 thousand hectares i.e. for

18.1% of total agricultural area. Gross value of agricultural production in 1977-78 was 2758 crores i.e. 8.2% of India (Total value of production in India being Rs. 33539 crores). Food production in Maharashtra increased from 60.72 lakh tonnes in 1959-60 to 109.50 lakh tonnes in 1983-84. However, Maharashtra is lagging in farm development—the cropping intensity is still very low due to lack of adequate irrigation, uneconomic size of holding, slow pace of utilisation of HYV seeds and technology and inadequate use of fertiliser etc. As a result, the productivity in many food crops in Maharashtra is lower than all India average. Green revolution which gave a boost to northern agriculture could not make inroad into Maharashtra.

Infrastructure

Maharashtra has achieved a substantial growth in infrastructural inputs. According to the Commerce Research Bureau, index of infrastructure development in 1981-82 was 116 (all India base=100) and occupied the top position.

Maharashtra is the most urbanised state in India. According to 1981 census 35% of its inhabitants reside in urban areas. Accelerated pace of urban growth in Maharashtra has significantly assisted the growth of industries in the state.

The state has well developed power sector. Power position—installation and generation—is quite substantial in the state. During 1984-85 the state accounted for 16.9% of the electricity generated in the country. Per capita power consumption in the state in 1984-85 was 280 KWH as against 143 KWH in India. The state generated 26,193 million KWH which was 16.7% of power generated in India in 1984-85.

The state has 180200 km. road length and 5297 km. railway route length. In terms of length of road and railway per 100 sq. km. the state's position was 13th and 15th respectively in 1982 and 1984.

Maharashtra has fairly well developed telephone and postal services. Telephone per 1000 of population was 11.9 in 1984 as against the national average of 4.7 and the population served by a Post Office in Maharashtra was 5341 in 1984, as against 4734 in India.

Maharashtra has got a very viable financial infrastructure. The Headquarters of many all India financial institutions and banks namely, R.B.I., I.D.B.I., I.C.I.C.I., L.I.C., U.T.I., G.I.C. and Commercial Banks like State Bank of India, Central Banks, Bank of

Maharashtra, Dena Bank, Bank of India etc. are located in Maharashtra. Cooperative Banking also well developed in the state. Available statistics indicate that by the end of December 1982, there were 4003 branches of commercial banks and the number of such branches per lakh of population was 6.4 (above the national average 6.0) per capita deposit and credit was Rs. 1494 and Rs. 1294 against national average of Rs. 765 and 522 respectively.

Maharashtra has made pioneering efforts to create industrial infrastructure by commissioning several agencies namely, State Industrial and Investment Corporation of Maharashtra (SICOM), Maharashtra Small Scale Industrial Development Corporation (MSSIDC), Maharashtra State Financial Corporation (MSFC), Maharashtra Industrial Development Corporation (MIDC), etc., while MIDC is involved in developing industrial land and providing basic infrastructure like water, drainage, industrial sheds and common facilities, MSFC and SICOM provides financial assistance, consultancy and related entrepreneurial support. MSSIDC is looking into the problems of small scale industrial with a view to create a viable and dynamic small scale industrial sector.

Industry

Maharashtra is the leading industrialised state in India having achieved considerable success in rate of industrial growth, diversification and structural change, dispersal and industrial movement in backward areas. Total fixed capital investment (in 1983-84) was highest in Maharashtra (Rs. 7500 crores) and the value of output in the same year was over Rs. 19,000 crores, the highest in any state in India. During 1982-83, the value added by manufacturing was Rs. 3601 crores (highest in India). During 1981-82, Maharashtra accounted for one sixth of aggregate productive capital of the country. According to the State Government statistics the number of working factories and average daily employment in June 1985 was 18608 and 1147 respectively. As per ASI data (1980-81) the state had highest percentage of factories (16.2%), factory employees (17.3%) and value added (25.0%) in India.

The important features of industrial development of the state are: there is a shift in favour of capital intensive industry, the industrial base primarily depending on chemical, capital goods and intermediary industries; about 66% of factories belong to non corporate sector, the cooperative sector account for 3% factories but the corporate sector which is dominated by the private limited companies contribute higher percentage employment, productive capital, value of output and productive capital.

Another important feature of the industrial development is lopsided growth and centralisation. So far the industrial activities remained concentrated in 3 districts namely Bombay, Thane and Pune, though of late, due to the State Government emphasise on industrial dispersal, there is a sign of spatial distribution. Though these 3 districts account for 25% of total population of the State, they together accounted for 70% of factories, 72% of employment, 69% of productive capital and 85% of value added in 1985. This centralised and concentrated development has created wide regional disparities. Most of the remaining districts are backward and have witnessed little development in industry. As per the Government of India's identification of backward districts, 17, (out of 30 districts) are backward (in all categories) which accounted for 54% of total area of the State and 39% of state population. However, it must be admitted that the State Government is fully conscious about the problem, and have initiated several successful policy measures through various state government agencies. Among these policy initiatives, the most important being industrial development in backward regions through promotion of entrepreneurship.

Uttar Pradesh[23]

Uttar Pradesh (U.P.) is the largest state in India in terms of population. According to 1981 census the population of U.P. was 1109 lakhs. U.P. is the fourth largest state in India in terms of area (294 thousand sq. kms.). In 1981, density of population was 377 persons per sq. km. and it ranked 4th in India. The state ranked 19th in terms of literacy (27%) and ranked 15th in urbanisation (18%). However, in spite of U.P.'s, vast population, natural resources and political power in Indian political administration, growth is very slow and the state is lagging behind even many minor states in India. For example, per capita income of the state in 1982-83 (at current price) was Rs. 1439 as against Indian average of Rs. 1891. Over the years, the share of U.P. in G.D.P. of India declined, while in 1970-71 U.P. contributed 12.47% to the Gross Domestic Product of India, this share declined to 11.90 in 1982-83 (at current prices). G.D.P. of U.P. in 1982-83 was Rs. 6085 crores as against Rs. 51119 crores in India.

The economy of the state is basically agrarian as 74% of total working force depend on agricultural occupation. The economy is heavily depended on agricultural sector can be seen from the fact that in 1982-83 agricultural sector produced 42.8% of Net State Domestic Product as against 33.5% in India, while the contribution manufacturing sector in India was 15.4%, manufacturing in U.P. contributed only 12.6% of Net S.D.P. The share of other sectors like construction, transport, banking, public administration and other services was also below the national average.

Agriculture

Agriculture continue to be the mainstay of the economy of U.P. as it provides employment to 72% of working population and contribute more than 42% to state domestic product.

The net cultivated area as percentage of total reporting area in U.P. in 1981-82 was 59.5% (4th in India) but the net irrigated areas as percentage net sown area was 10.5% and ranked 22nd among Indian states. Gross value of agricultural products accounted for Rs. 5158 crores which was 8.2% value of agricultural products in India in 1977-78. In regard to average yield of major crops U.P. remained at the low level when compared with India.

Poor performance of agriculture in U.P. was due to the low intensity of irrigation, small size of holdings, excessive pressure on agricultural land, and absence of utilisation of modern implements and inputs by small sized agriculturists, etc.

Infrastructure

The contribution of transport, banking and service sector is an indication of slow growth of infrastructural development in U.P. According to Commerce Research Bureau calculation, the index of infrastructure development in U.P. was 114 and ranked 8th among Indian states. Urbanisation which is a crucial factor is very slow in U.P. According to 1981 census, only 18.1% of state population was urban inhabitants against the all India average of 23.7%.

Installed capacity of power generation in U.P. in 1984-85 was 5165 MW, (which was 12.4% of the country) but the state generated 16739 million KWH, i.e., 10.7% of the total power generated in the country. U.P. is a deficit state. In 1984-85 the deficit was 13.2% of total requirement. Per capita aggregate power consumption in the state was 89 KWH as against 143 KWH in India. Per capita industrial consumption of power was 35 KWH in the state, much below the national average of 87 KWH.

In respect of road and railway length the state ranked 15th and 8th respectively having 52 km. road length per 100 sq. km. and 30 km. railway route length per 1000 sq. km. Postal and telephone services also not very developed, average population served by a post office in U.P. was 6115 as against national average of 4734 and the telephone connection per thousand of population was 1.7 against the national average of 4.7.

U.P. is also lagging in respect of financial infrastructure. Available data indicate that by the end of December 1982, that there were 5122 branches of commercial banks, i.e. 4.6 branches per lakh of population while the average number of branches per lakh of population was 6.0 per capita deposit and bank credit in U.P. was 471 and Rs. 222 respectively against average of Rs. 765 and Rs. 522 respectively.

Industrial Development

The State has been lagging in industrial development in spite of huge natural resources and abundant manpower. Relative progress of the state in industrial development can be seen from the A.S.I. data 1980-81. The data indicate that U.P. ranked 5th with 7151 factories, 4th with 770626 employees, 5th with output of Rs. 377662 lakhs and 5th with value added of Rs. 74930 lakhs. As per the data of Directorate of Industries, Government of U.P. large and medium sector industries (registered under Factories Act) in private sector increased from 257 in 1972 to 350 in 1983. However, investment increased from 392.97 crores to 1250.53 crores. Production increased from Rs. 649.26 crores to Rs. 2316.07 crores and employment increased from 171820 to 228571 during the above period. The number of small scale industries, investment and employment increased from 3679 to 5154, Rs. 55.72 crores to 200.55 crores and 119001 to 239186 persons.

The major large scale industries in U.P. in terms of value added are food and food products (17%) chemical and chemical products (9%), basic metal and alloys (6%), cotton textiles (12%), electricity (14%) and other (42%). The estimate share of private sector in total industrial investment in the state was 57% in 1984-85 which indicate role of private sector in U.P. is not as significant as in Maharashtra.

Another important aspect of industrial development is regional imbalance in growth of industries. Most of the industrial activities are concentrated in Kanpur, Allahabad and Ghaziabad. Overall economic development in U.P. is very uneven and lopsided. Out of 5 regions Western, Central, Eastern, Bundelkhand and Hill regions, 3 regions, namely Hill, Bundelkhand and Eastern regions have been declared as backward by the state government.

Central Government has identified 41 districts (out of 57) as backward districts which consists of 70% of state area and 63% of state population, which indicate that there is a serious imbalance in development in U.P.

However, in order to remove the several infrastructural bottlenecks and to create a favourable climate for industrial growth, the state government has commissioned several agencies like Pradeshiya Industrial and Investment Corporation of U.P. (PICUP) — which caters to the financial need of large and medium industries and promote joint sector venture, Uttar Pradesh Industrial Development Corporation (UPSIDC) — which provides infrastructural support, Uttar Pradesh Financial Corporation (UPFC) — caters to the financial need of small and medium industries, Uttar Pradesh Small Industries Corporation provides marketing raw materials and other services to small scale industries. There are other state level agencies instituted with a view to promote entrepreneurs and industries in the state and in particularly in backward areas.

REFERENCES

1. Glery Shirokov, 'The Industrial Revolution in the East', Progress Publishers, Moscow (1985), p. 92.
2. A.I. Medovoy, 'The Indian Economy', Progress Publishers, Moscow, 1984.
3. Government of India, Resolution on Industrial Policy (6th April 1948).
4. D.R. Gadgil, 'Experience of Indian Planning' (Writings and Speeches of Dr. Gadgil on Planning and Development), Gokhale Institute of Economics and Politics, Poona.
5. The Approach to the Fifth Five Year Plan, Planning Commission, Govt. of India.
6. Govt. of India, Industrial Policy Resolution (30th April 1956).
7. Govt. of India, Industrial Policy Resolution, 1948.
8. Statement of Industrial Policy made by George Fernandes, Minister of Industry, in the Parliament on 23rd December 1977.
9. Industrial Policy Statement, July 23, 1980.
10. Draft Seventh Five Year Plan, Planning Commission, Govt. of India, 1985.

11. Govt. of India, 'Report of the Working Group on Identification of Backward Areas', Planning Commission, New Delhi, 1969.

12. Govt. of India, 'Report on Fiscal and Financial Incentives for Development of Industries in Backward Areas', Ministry of Industry, New Delhi, 1969.

13. Govt. of India, 'Report on Industrial Dispersal', National Committee on the Development of Backward Areas', Planning Commission, New Delhi, 1981.

14. As announced by the Govt. of India, Ministry of Industries, Development of Industrial Development, 29th April 1986.

15. S. Chakraborty, 'Aspects of India's Development, Strategy for 1980's, in Facets of India's Development', Published by the Industrial Credit and Investment Corporation of India Ltd., Bombay, 1986.

16. V.K.R.V. Rao, 'India's National Income in 1999-2000 AD' in Economic Times Silver Jubilee Issue, dated 19th December 1986.

17. A.M. Khusro, 'Strategy for Rural Development' in 'Facets of India's Development', Published by Industrial Credit and Investment Corporation of India Ltd., Bombay, 1986.

18. Quoted from 'Growth and Equity in Agriculture' an article by M.L. Dantwala in Economic Times (Silver Jubilee Issue), dated 19th December 1986.

19. Government of India, Economic Survey, 1986-87.

20. C. Rangarajan, 'Recent Trends in Industrial Growth' in 'Development News', Vol. 5, 1984, IDBI, Bombay.

21. Govt. of India, Economic Survey, 1986-87.

22. & 23. Data in this sections have been used from several publications namely, Basic Statistics on State Economies of India (Commerce Research Bureau, Bombay) Economic Survey, Govt. of India, RBI Bulletins, Hand Book of Basic Statistics (Govt. of Maharashtra) and several other publications of Govt. of Maharashtra. Data also gathered from Financial Express, Business Standard and Economic Times particularly Silver Jubilee Issue dated March 6, 1987 and several other publications.

3

INSTITUTIONAL EFFORTS TO DEVELOP ENTREPRENEURSHIP IN INDIA

Introduction

Colonial Policy of plunders and obstructions to economic development of India not only delayed the industrial development and economic growth but also restricted the natural growth of entrepreneurship. British policy created adverse socio-psychological, economic and political condition and initiatives of Indian entrepreneurs were neither welcomed nor naturally permissible. Colonial Policy did not encourage independent development of industries which could threat the British industrial interest in India and world market. They simply wanted to serve the British interest by keeping India as a supplier of cheap raw materials to British industries and market for British goods.

Private enterprise in India was started by Britisher during the early 19th century with a view to supply the raw materials to British industries. Indian industries were simply processing industries (during the early 19th century). Colonial Policy had already caused a blow to indigenous craft and disintegrated the link between agriculture and craft with an aim to eliminate indigenous entrepreneurial initiator. However, in spite of calculated move of colonialists, some Indians enter into the field of industry and joined the rank of entrepreneurship in the middle of 19th century. Parsis, Marwaries, Jains, Chettiers started industrial ventures and gained strength by the close of the century. Development and growth of Managing Agency system in India had further strengthen the position of Indian entrepreneurs. Through the system of Managing Agency, some Indian business houses gained monopoly power. Industrial houses, which have emerged as monopolists in post independent India through Managing Agency system are Tatas, Birlas, Dalmias, Singhanias, etc.

Another aspect of development of Indian entrepreneurship during British period is the concentration of indigenous entrepreneurs in western India. The strength of western (Indian) business community according to R. Mukherjee[1] was primarily due to—

(i) the greater percentage of capital under their control, and
(ii) greater degree of collaboration between Indian and European business community.

Causes of Slow Growth

Faster growth of entrepreneurship depends on the favourable social-cultural-economic and political factors, which were absent in India during British rule. We would like to mention about some immediate factors restricting the growth of entrepreneurs.

I. Restrictions on Social Mobility

Indian society was based on rigid caste system which restricted the social mobility in Hindu society. Indian craft, which was main form of entrepreneurship was hereditary. Therefore, the restriction on social mobility reduced the scope of expansion of entrepreneurship.

II. Disintegration of Indian Craft

Craft was primary form of enterprise before the advent of British in India. Entrepreneurial activities were based on various types of crafts. However, establishment of colonial rule destroyed the Indian crafts. India became a market for British products and a supplier of cheap raw materials to British industries. Destruction of craft caused a blow to the progress of craft base entrepreneurship.

III. Agrarian System

Indian handicraft flourished due to closer ties between handicraft and agriculture and due to the system of community as a production unit. But the colonial agrarian system, particularly the imposition of land tax dealt a serious blow to the community system and greater part of peasants were turned into tenants of Zamindars and lost their economic independence. They were forced to produce according to dictates of landlords or money-lenders. As a result, independent profession like craft was damaged and entrepreneurship reached to a point of stagnation.

IV. Protected Customs Duties

Very high customs Duties on Indian goods (70 to 80% on their value) were introduced to protect British industry whereas, the British goods in Calcutta paid duty of 2.5% of the price of products in Calcutta in 1820.[2]

British tariff policy between 1929 and 1933 adversely affected many Indian industries. Preferential duties also made British goods cheaper in Indian market. All these measures made the Indian goods less competitive and Indian business less profitable which killed the entrepreneurial initiatives of Indians.

V. Banking

Banking in India started with the establishment of first Presidential bank in Calcutta in 1806 and subsequently in Madras and Bombay. Big British Banks entered in India by the middle of 19th century. They were acting as semi-Government institutions and implementing Government's Colonial Policy. They were controlling external trade as well as domestic business through colonial financing policy. They were primarily following the colonial policy to finance British trade and industries. Indian entrepreneurs were deprived of funds. Therefore, lack of banking support hindered the growth of Indian enterprise.

VI. Development Policy

Colonial Government followed a policy of perpetual suppression of development of India. No activities for independent economic development was undertaken in India. Whatever industries were encouraged to develop were light industries. Development of heavy industries and industrial infrastructure were totally absent. Lack of infrastructure was also a disincentives to Indian traders, businessmen and money-lenders to start manufacturing.

Institutional Framework

According to Staley and Morse[3] fostering vigorous entrepreneurship development in underdeveloped country requires that :

1. Overall environmental setting must be one which provides stability and adequate level of reward for private business initiative.

2. A well functioning system of price signals which accurately reflects societies economic needs.
3. A positive programme to aid emerging small sector entrepreneurs.
4. Upgradation of skills, increased access to important technological and market knowledge to benefit from better qualities, less expensive factor inputs by means of institutional arrangement.

The above factors, which determine the growth of entrepreneurship depends on the well framed growth oriented economic policy. However, during British period, economic policy was a part of political design of colonial exploitation of India. After Independence, Governments in India, attempted to reframe economic policy for faster economic development of the country. Since entrepreneurs play the key role in industrial and economic development, measures have been initiated to create environment for faster development of entrepreneurship. These measures have induced industrial investment in various priority areas like rural and backward regions.

The Government has also taken steps to assist the potential entrepreneurs through several positive programmes. These programmes aimed at increasing the access to financial capital, technical know-how, market information, provision of cheaper factor inputs and technical consultancy; arrangement of training, etc. for entrepreneurs. Several institutions have been established at the all India and state level to render the above services to the old and new entrepreneurs. However, we shall limit our discussions to institutions which are playing very significant role to promote first generation entrepreneurs (new entrepreneurs). These are the development banks, entrepreneurship development institutions and technical consultancy organisations. While the entrepreneurship development institutions are engaged in identification, selection and training of potential entrepreneurs, the technical consultancy organisations in addition to industrial consultancy provide entrepreneurship training. The Development Banks on the other hand provide vital inputs like financial capital & development assistance.

Development Banking Institutions

One of the most important developments in the post-Independence India is the establishment of several specialised financial and non-financial institution to hasten the process of industrial development in general and promotion of entrepreneurship in particular. Private industrial investment in India was not only concentrated in few hands but also that investment was concentrated at few industrially developed centres. Therefore, there was the need to mobilise public savings, to disperse industrial investment to less developed regions and to ensure supply of financial inputs to potential entrepreneurs. The government has therefore established several financial institutions and also nationalised private institutions to attain the above objectives. In course of time several all India and state level development banks, investment institutions and specialised institutions have come up. At present there are 3 all India Development Banks namely, Industrial Finance Corporation of India (established in 1948), Industrial Credit and Investment Corporation of India (Set up in 1955) and Industrial Development Banks of India set up in 1964. There are 3 investment institutions namely, Life Insurance Corporation of India (established in 1956), Unit Trust of India (established in 1964) and General Insurance Corporation of India (established in 1973). These institutions particularly 3 development banks provide long and medium term loan to industries. They also provide other development banking services.

In 1951 State Financial Corporation Act was passed and State Financial Corporations were established in the states to provide short and medium term loans to industries particularly in small scale sector. Another state level institutions namely State Industrial Development Corporations were established to promote medium scale industries and joint sector. At present there are 18 SFCs and 28 SIDCs.

There are few more specialised institutions like Industrial Reconstruction Bank of India (I.R.B.I.). In fact it is not a new organisation. Industrial Reconstruction Corporation of India (I.R.C.I.), which was established in 1971 to look after sick industries was renamed as I.R.B.I. in 1985. Export-Import Bank of India was established in March 1982 to extend assistance for promotion of export. In 1955, National Small Industries Development Corporation was established to extend support to small industries. At the state level there are state small industries 'development corporations, established to manage industrial estates, to supply raw materials, etc. All these state level institutions are providing various assistance and services to the industries, but special attention is being given to the industries coming up in backward regions and the units established by the new entrepreneurs. It can be seen from the sanction and disbursement of institutional finance, that the financial institutions are playing a very crucial role to promote industrialization. It is also very significant to note that out of cumulative sanction of Rs. 39,402.43 crores, Rs. 16,522.34 crores went to backward areas, and out of cumulative disbursement of Rs. 29,153.43 crores, of Rs. 12,112.27 crores, went to backward areas, i.e. 41.9% and 41.6% of total sanction and disbursement went to industries in backward regions. (Please see Appendix iv & v for details).

Among the All India Financial Institutions IDBI, IFCI and ICICI take special interest in promoting entrepreneurship particularly in backward areas and rural centres through assistance to various institutions conducting EDP and by rendering concessional financial assistance to new entrepreneurs. They also actively support to other institutions like TCOs, National Science and Technology Entrepreneurship Development Board (NSTEDB), Entrepreneurship Development Institute of India (EDII) and other agencies. So far, with IDBIS support 447 EDPs were conducted by these institutes and 12,200 entrepreneurs were trained. IDBI, as a measures of post training support to trained entrepreneurs provides 2/3 of cost of service rendered by TCOs. IDBI, in order to encourage rural and tiny enterprises render financial support to selected voluntary agencies. Another important step taken by IDBI to encourage entrepreneurship among science and technology graduates through setting up of 'Science and Technological Entrepreneurship Parks' (STEPs). Two such parts are at Ranchi in Bihar and one in Maharashtra.

IFCI, in addition to participating with IDBI & ICICI directly provides support by Risk Capital assistance to first generation (new) entrepreneurs, though Risk Capital Foundation (RCF) sponsored by IFCI in 1975. Under this scheme interest free personal loans from Rs. 15 lakhs to Rs. 30 lakhs given to the first generation new entrepreneurs to meet a part of promoters contribution for setting up medium sized units. Under the RCF's scheme 170 entrepreneurs have been assisted and Rs. 1025.34 lakhs has been sanctioned till June 1986.

IDBI also operates (through SFCs) Seed Capital Scheme for technically qualified entrepreneurs in small scale sector to meet a part of promoters equity capital.

Another important step taken by IDBI to promote and assist the small entrepreneurs is the formation of Small Industries Development Fund (SIDF). Among other objectives, the fund will render equity support to small and tiny industries through its special capital and seed capital scheme. Special concessions will be given to the women, SC/ST and physically handicapped entrepreneurs. SIDF will also finance activities to identify new industrial activities and to train and develop entrepreneurs in small scale sector.

In addition to the above, the state level financial institutions (SFCs) and development institution (SIDCs) are also rendering financial assistance to new industries set up by first generation entrepreneurs particularly by women, SC/ST and physically handicapped entrepreneurs. SFCs and SIDCs also provide equity capital to the competent and needy entrepreneurs under special capital scheme and seed capital scheme. According to the Report on Development Banking (1986-87), the cumulative assistance sanctioned by SFCs and SIDFs till 31.3.87 was Rs. 9343.1 crores and the risk capital to industries under seed capital scheme (by SIDCs) was Rs. 59.8 crores for 811 projects (for details please see Appendix vi,vii,viii & ix).

Entrepreneurship Development Institutions

Increasing access to financial resources no doubt is a necessary supporting factor for development of entrepreneurship but not the sufficient factor. Potential entrepreneurs should be identified, trained and motivated to start their own industrial units. The scientific development programme which covers the above areas is called Entrepreneurship Development Programme(E.D.P.). E.D.P. has been nicely defined by S.M. Palia as a 'programme designed to help a person in strengthening his entrepreneurial motive and in acquiring skills and capabilities necessary for playing his entrepreneurial role effectively. Towards this end it is necessary to promote his understanding of motives, motivation pattern, their impact on behaviour and entrepreneurial value.'[4] A programme which seeks to do this can qualify to be called an EDP.

Entrepreneurship Development Programme (EDP) in India is of recent origins yet a number of private and government institutions are engaged in conducting E.D.P. The lead in this direction (of E.D.P.) was taken by the Small Industries Development Organisation (SIDO) in sixties through establishment of Small Industries Extension & Training Institute (SIET) at Hyderabad. Small Industries Service Institutes (SISI) also conduct E.D.P. at various states. In 1978, State Bank of India introduced E.D.Ps. However the most important step

District Level Institution		
DIC	RDC	
DRDA	VA	

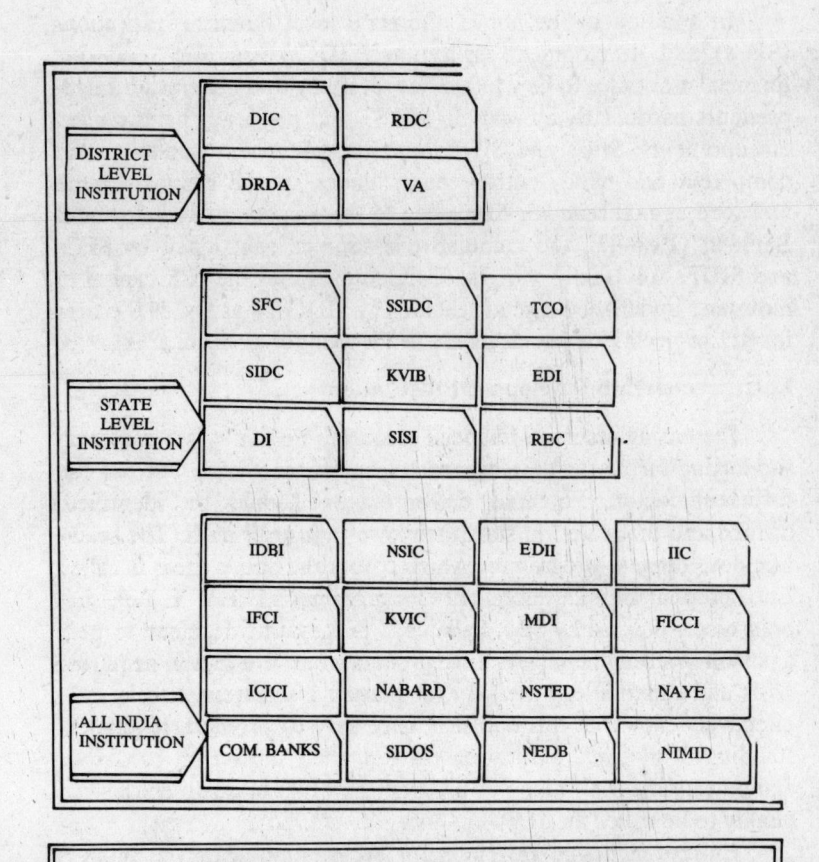

State Level Institution		
SFC	SSIDC	TCO
SIDC	KVIB	EDI
DI	SISI	REC

All India Institution			
IDBI	NSIC	EDII	IIC
IFCI	KVIC	MDI	FICCI
ICICI	NABARD	NSTED	NAYE
COM. BANKS	SIDOS	NEDB	NIMID

MAJOR INSTITUTIONS/ORGANISATIONS ENGAGED IN EDP IN INDIA

FIG - 1

was taken by Gujarat 'Centre for Entrepreneurship Development' (C.E.D.) which was established in 1979, 'India Investment Centre' (I.I.C.) and Zavier Institute of Social Services also conducts E.D.P. A boost to E.D.P. and consultancy was given by the All India Financial Institutes — I.D.B.I., I.F.C.I. & I.C.I.C.I. through establishment of technical consultancy organisations (TCOs). Now let us examine the activities of some of these organizations.

(i) Gujarat E.D.P.

In India, the Gujarat E.D.P. is the longest operating programme of its kind. The Gujarat experiment started with the introduction of a scheme in 1969 called Technicians Scheme by Gujarat Industrial Investment Corporation (GIIC) under which technically qualified persons with viable projects were eligible for concessional loan at attractive term. The scheme was quite successful. The scheme was expanded into New Entrepreneurs Scheme (N.E.S.) in 1969 under which all the new entrepreneurs were entitled for the assistance. Apart from G.I.I.C., Gujarat State Financial Corporation (G.S.F.C.) also a partner of the scheme under the leadership of G.I.I.C. This scheme was also very successful.

Being encouraged by the success of N.E.S., the Gujarat Corporation introduced a programme to identify and develop new entrepreneurs through training and motivational programme. The rational of the Gujarat E.D.P. as Dr. Patel stated "that many employees in industry and commerce, workers, supervisors, merchants and salesmen and a number of young engineers and graduates had latent entrepreneurial talents and a desire or capacity to be self employed. Many lacked self confidence to come forward to their own ventures. Their enterprise was not fully developed, the motivation to take risk despite the frustrations of their current occupation was not strong enough. Some needed opportunity counselling, others knowledge of how to establish and manage an industrial enterprise. If a comprehensive entrepreneurship development programme could meet these needs and fill the information motivation and skill gaps, it was argued that many new entrepreneurs might be developed and made competent to successfully set up and operate industrial enterprise."[5]

On the basis of the above assumptions Gujarat E.D.P. designed to draw industrially and commercially experienced technicians, traders, managers, salesmen, professional and educated unemployed to give them low cost high quality training. In the words of V.G.

Patel, "qualitatively, it is recognized as the most comprehensive development programme for entrepreneurs in India, combining sophisticated entrepreneur selection techniques, development inputs, including behavioural psychological (motivation) training and business management counselling and culminating in the preparation of a project proposal by each trainee for his industrial unit."[6]

The major objectives of EDP in Gujarat are (i) to identify and train potential entrepreneurs, (ii) developing entrepreneurial capabilities, (iii) imparting basic managerial understanding, and (iv) post training assistance. In fact Gujarat has developed a comprehensive programme consisting of identification and training of potential entrepreneurs, post training counselling and arrangements of finance and infrastructural facilities. As a result of combined efforts of G.I.I.C., G.S.F.C. and other State Government organisation, EDP experience is quite successful.

By the end of 1981 Gujarat C.E.D. has trained 4263 new entrepreneurs through 171 programmes conducted in 71 centres. By 1984, 1476 entrepreneurs had established their units while 1074 were in the process of starting. One of the important feature is the spread of training centres at small towns. Gujarat experiment has proved that a good response through E.D.P. can be received if the programme is well designed and nurtured.

(ii) **Other C.E.D./I.E.D.**

Gujarat experiment has encouraged the other states and Financial Institutes to establish such centres to promote entrepreneurs through scientific training. In U.P., a Institute of Entrepreneurship Development (I.E.D.) has been jointly established by the All India Financial Institutions and the Government of Uttar Pradesh at Lucknow in March 1986. The broad objectives of the Institute are:

(a) To organise training research and extension activities towards the development of potential and existing entrepreneurs.
(b) To coordinate and support E.D.Ps. in the State and its adjoining areas particularly in the underdeveloped regions.
(c) To train trainers, counsellors and motivators involved in the development of entrepreneurship.
(d) To activate the media towards entrepreneurship and help create conclusive entrepreneurial climate for the growth and development of entrepreneurs.

(e) To help provide information support to the institutions engaged in the promotion of entrepreneurship.

Upto April 1987, the I.E.D. has completed 13 programmes and trained 380 persons.

C.E.D./I.E.D. also being established in Orissa and Bihar. These centres will focus attention to the development of entrepreneurs in backward areas.

(iii) **Entrepreneurship Development Institute of India (E.D.I.I.)**

Entrepreneurship Development Institute of India (EDII) at Ahmedabad has been established by the All India Financial Institution, State Bank and State Government is the apex institute for EDPs in India. This Institute has been established as principal agency for creating the institutional infrastructure for entrepreneurship development. This institution will run model training programme, train the trainers, conduct research and help the state level agencies in planning, implementing and monitoring E.D.Ps. With the establishment of E.D.I.I. a long felt need to establish an institute to coordinate the various E.D.P. activities has been fulfilled. During 1985-86, E.D.I.I. has conducted 4 E.D.Ps. and undertaken 2 research projects.

(iv) **India Investment Centre (I.I.C.)**

India Investment Centre also took active interest to develop entrepreneurship through its Entrepreneurial Guidance Bureau (E.G.B.). They conducted E.D.P. in various parts of the country, particularly in backward regions with close cooperation of State and Central agencies. The target groups of E.D.P. conducted by I.I.C. usually are qualified engineers, diploma holders or science graduates with applied physics or chemistry. The programme comprises of:

(a) identification and selection of potential entrepreneurs,
(b) developing entrepreneurial capabilities for playing entrepreneurial role effectively,
(c) equipping them with basic managerial knowledge, and
(d) assisting them to establish their own projects.

The I.I.C. first conducted its E.D.P. at Calcutta in 1974-75 since then it had conducted number of E.D.Ps. through E.G.B. till it was taken over by I.D.B.I. in 1982.

(v) Xavier Institute of Social Service

Xavier Institute of Social Service at Ranchi is a voluntary organisation. Since early seventies this organisation is engaged in imparting training to tiny village entrepreneurs particularly to tribals and other backward people. The programme conducted by XISS is quite successful and about 50% of trained people have started their units in trade, clothing, repairs, etc. This Institute has also extended cooperation to set-up Rural Entrepreneurship Development Institute by I.D.B.I. for training to rural entrepreneurs.

(vi) Development Banking Centre (D.B.C.)

D.B.C. at New Delhi is basically an institute to promote Development Banking through training and research but it has paid considerable attention also to promote entrepreneurship. D.B.Cs primary concern lies in the development and application of Science and Technology for developing entrepreneurship. The major operation objectives followed by D.B.C. are :

(a) Train the trainers.
(b) Conduct training for entrepreneurs in varied locals.
(c) Develop new materials for training of trainers.
(d) Develop new trainers to conduct Entrepreneurship Management Programmes (E.M.P.).
(e) Conduct research on Entrepreneurship Development.

From the above it can be seen that the major focus of D.B.C. is to promote well equipped trained personnel for carrying out the task of entrepreneurship training or E.D.P.

(vii) Small Industries Service Institutes (S.I.S.I.)

S.I.S.I. is also playing a very vital role in the field of training of engineering science graduates and diploma holders.

They also conduct training in collaboration with engineering colleges and other agencies in various states. The programme is confined to freshers and jobless. The success ratio is usually 10 to 15%.

Technical Consultancy Organisations

Like finance and training, consultancy service is also an important input for entrepreneurship development. Access to high quality consultancy services improve the operational efficiency of entrepreneurs and increase the productivity of the industrial units. However, before seventies there was no such organisation for the small entrepreneurs where low cost consultancy was available. Therefore financial institution (I.D.B.I., I.F.C.I. and I.C.I.C.I.) took initiative to set up such organizations and the first T.C.O., viz. The Kerala Industrial and Technical Consultancy Ltd. in 1972 in Kerala. By the end of June 1986, there were 17 T.C.Os promoted by All India Financial Institutions. Out of 17, 8 are under the lead of I.D.B.I., 5 are under the lead of I.F.C.I., 3 are under the lead of I.C.I.C.I. and one promoted by the Government of Karnataka.

The major objectives of the T.C.Os are to provide a comprehensive package of services to small entrepreneurs, promoting entrepreneurship and rendering consultancy assistance to the State Government for industrial development. The main functions of such T.C.Os are to—

(a) identification of industrial potential,
(b) conduct pre-investment studies and prepare project report feasibility studies,
(c) undertake techno-economic survey,
(d) undertake market research, and
(e) identify potential entrepreneurs and provide them with technical and managerial assistance.

In the field of training T.C.Os identify potential entrepreneurs, train them and render post training counselling and guidance in selecting project, preparation of project profile and establishing their own units.

During the year 1985-86 (June-July) the T.C.Os took up 1537 feasibility studies, 867 project profiles/appraisals, 225 surveys, 31 turn key assignments and 121 rehabilitation/diagnostic studies. During 1986-87, T.C.Os have completed 3148 pre-investment and 205 post investment assignments.

During (1986-87) the T.C.Os have conducted 142 entrepreneurial development programmes and trained 3653 potential entrepreneurs. As on 30.6.1987, the T.C.Os in India have completed 591 E.D.Ps throughout the country and have trained 16685 potential entrepreneurs. In the state of U.P., the U.P. Industrial Consultants Ltd. (established in 1974) has completed 86 E.D.P. and trained 2885 potential entrepreneurs while in the state of Maharashtra, Maharashtra Industrial and Technical Consultancy Organisation Ltd. (MITCON) established in 1985-86 have conducted 17 E.D.P. and trained 432 potential entrepreneurs.

Though the T.C.Os are relatively young organisations and yet to overcome the teething troubles, they are well set to fill the gap in the field of consultancy for industrial and entrepreneurship development in India.

State Level Incentives to Entrepreneurs

In addition to the all India Institutions and incentives (and subsidies) helping promotion of entrepreneurship and industrial development, there are many schemes of incentives introduced by the State Governments to hasten the process of entrepreneurship development in the States. State Government have also commissioned several institutions to implement the schemes of 'incentives/subsidies and other necessary assistance to the entrepreneurs. In this section, we shall examine, in brief, the state level institutions and incentives in Uttar Pradesh (U.P.) and Maharashtra.

Uttar Pradesh

U.P. has witnessed very slow progress in industrial development in spite of having abundant manpower and natural resources. The main objective of industrial policy of the State to promote spatially distributed industrial development. The primary focus is on the exploitation of local resources through locally developed entrepreneurship. The state government has, therefore commissioned several state level institutions and introduced its own scheme of incentives for promoting entrepreneurship and industries. The important institutions are:

(a) U.P. State Industrial Development Corporation Ltd. (UPSIDC).
(b) The Pradeshiya Industrial and Investment Corporation of Uttar Pradesh (PICUP).
(c) U.P. Financial Corporation (UPFC).
(d) U.P. Small Industries Corporation (UPSIC).

In addition to the above, there are several other State Government Corporations attending to the needs of individual industries, and in the process assist the upcoming entrepreneurs.

UPSIDC

Established by the State Government for accelerating the pace of industrial growth. The major functions of UPSIDC are:

(i) Acquisition of land for industrial purpose and development of infrastructure.
(ii) Setting up of medium and heavy industries in joint sector.
(iii) Financial assistance to medium and heavy industries in joint sector through equity participation and underwriting.
(iv) Consultancy services.

The corporation is the primary institution to acquire and develop land for industries. It also develops roads, drainage, water, etc. State Government has also constructed industrial sheds in the industrial areas. These sheds are given to new entrepreneurs at the concessional rate. UPSIDC has already developed 40 industrial areas in the State.

PICUP

PICUP has been created by the State Government to promote medium and large scale industries primarily by extending financial assistance and other catalytic services. The following services are provided by PICUP.

(i) Financial services,
(ii) Technical Services,
(iii) Institutional Support.

PICUP provides secured term loans to medium and large industries, underwrite shares.

On behalf of IDBI, PICUP provides Seed Capital to the Entrepreneurs and also help the industries by leasing equipment for modernization, expansion or diversification.

PICUP extends entrepreneurial support to first generation entrepreneurs — technocrats, competent professionals etc. by providing 'Risk Capital' under IDBI's Seed Capital Scheme and Risk Capital Foundation's risk capital scheme and UPSIDC's equity participation scheme. Seed capital are provided to entrepreneurs in SSI sector who undertake expansion, diversification of SSI units, who intend to graduate from SSI to medium scale sector, those who are in medium scale and wants to expand/diversify their units and who wants to take over sick units.

It also provides various technical and managerial and other services to the entrepreneurs through its Udyog Bandhu.

UPFC

UPFC is engaged in extending financial capital to the small and medium scale industries in the State. The major function of UPFC are:

(i) Extending term loan assistance for setting up industries in small and medium scale sector.
(ii) Composite Loan to artisans.
(iii) Providing soft loan to cover equity gap to help small scale units being set up in backward regions.
(iv) Providing loan on concessional rate to the sick industries.
(v) Providing assistance to industries in small scale and decentralised sector as also to the units set up in hills and backward regions.

Concessional rate of interest is charged on the loans given to new entrepreneur—particularly in backward and hill regions.

UPSIC

UPSIC is engaged in promoting small scale industries in the State. The major function of UPSIC are:

(i) Procurement and distribution of raw materials.
(ii) Supply of machinery on hire purchase.
(iii) Operating of import assistance scheme.
(iv) Participation in joint venture.
(v) Providing marketing assistance to small scale industries.

The Corporation procure and supply various types of imported or indigenous critical raw materials like steel, iron, copper, soda pesticides, acids, coal, coke etc. The Corporation also assist the entrepreneurs to acquire industrial equipments and machines on higher purchase basis. Entrepreneurs can also avail financial assistance for importing machineries. UPSIC also provides marketing guidance and assistance to small scale industries. Exemption from security money is given for Government purchase. UPSIC also release 90% payment in case of Government supply. There is also reservation of some items to be purchased exclusively from SSI units. 15% price preferences as compared to large units is given to SSI.

The Corporation also promote joint sector small scale units to help the educated unemployed entrepreneurs. It also provides capital and equity shares with regional development corporations apart from rendering managerial and technical services to the entrepreneurs.

State Subsidies

Apart from various incentives and subsidies of the State Government agencies mentioned above, there are few more incentives to the entrepreneurs in the State. These are :

State Capital Subsidy, various types of assistance like interest subsidy, consultancy subsidy, power subsidy, generating set subsidy, stamp duty subsidy etc., are given to entrepreneurs. For tiny and small scale units upto 4% interest subsidy, 100% consultancy subsidy, upto 9 paise (per unit) power subsidy are provided under the marginal money scheme. The Government also provides upto 10% margin money to tiny and small scale units.

Special concessions are given to Pioneer and Prestige industries. A pioneer industry is one which is set up in zero industry Tehsil where there is no unit having investment of Rs. one crore or more. A pioneer industry receive special capital subsidy of 15% (max. Rs. 15 lacs) in case it is in a zero industry Tehsil which does not qualify for central subsidy. A 5% subsidy (max. Rs. 5 lacs) is available if the unit is established in 10% central capital subsidy districts. In 18 districts, such industries receive sales tax exemption. A Pioneer unit can also opt for sales tax different in lieu of exemption.

A prestige unit is one which is set up with an investment of Rs. 25 crores or more. A prestige unit receive all the concessions and incentives available to a Pioneer industry. A Prestige unit also receive State Capital subsidy of 15% in case they set up ancilliary industry in conformity with the Government of India norms of nucleus projects.

Maharashtra

Maharashtra is the most industrialised state in India but the development that has been achieved by the state has been localised in 2/3 pockets, namely Bombay, Pune, and Thane. Lack of spatial distribution of industries caused the serious regional imbalances in the development. Therefore the industrial policy of Maharashtra based on 2 important objects viz., (a) reduce concentration of industries through dispersal, and (b) to promote industries in relatively less developed regions.

In order to achieve the above objectives, Maharashtra has commissioned many state level institutions and introduced state level subsidies for the entrepreneurs particularly for first generation entrepreneurs specially in backward regions. The important agencies are :

(i) Maharashtra Industrial Development Corporation (MIDC).
(ii) Maharashtra State Financial Corporation (MSFC).
(iii) Maharashtra Small Scale Industries Development Corporation (MSSIDC).
(iv) The State Industrial and Investment Corporation of Maharashtra (SICOM).
(v) Maharashtra Agro Industries Development Corporation.

In addition to the above there are 4 regional development corporations for 4 regions namely Vidharbha, Marathwada, Western Maharashtra and Konkon. While the first five corporations are state level corporations, the last four attend the specific regional problems.

MIDC

MIDC perform the most crucial function of supplying necessary infrastructure to the industries. As an input supplier, it develop industrial areas, constructs roads, industrial sheds and arrange for water and electric supply etc. It gives special incentives to new entrepreneurs and backward areas. MIDC has so far developed more than 70 industrial areas, out of which 55 are in the developing parts.

MSFC

MSFC provides financial inputs to the small and medium industries and offer special incentives to the industries in backward regions. Special concession is also given to industries promoted by technically qualified and educated unemployed. The important schemes for young entrepreneurs are :

(a) Scheme for Educated Unemployed : Those who have passed the

Institutional Efforts to Develop Entrepreneurship in India

10th standard or ITI trained and have registered their names with employment exchange are entitled for financial assistance at concessional rate.

(b) Young Technicians Assistance Scheme : The scheme has been designed for Technicians like drillers, welders, turners, carpenters etc. The loan is advanced up to Rs 2 lacs with lower margin.

(c) Technicians Assistance Scheme : Those technicians who are degree and/or diploma holders are entitled for loan upto Rs 5 lacs.

(d) Composite Loan Scheme : Composite loan upto Rs 25000 is granted to artisans or village industries.

MSFC also offer several other incentives and concessions to the first generation entrepreneurs.

SICOM

SICOM is the most successful among the state level industrial investment corporation. It is the main institution catering to the needs of large and medium industries and promoting joint sector industries in Maharashtra. It is also the important state Government institution to disperse industries from the congested Bombay - Thane - Pune region. SICOM perform the following major functions :

(a) Project identification, investment guidance and plant location.
(b) Arranging finance and subsidies for the industries.
(c) Providing industrial escort services (after sales services).
(d) Provide equipment leasing, etc.

For new entrepreneurs SICOM provides Seed Capital (of IDBI). Professionally qualified entrepreneurs such as technicians, qualified/experienced managers and manager experienced in other industrial disciplines are eligible for seed capital.

SICOM also provides Merchant Banking Services—subscribe directly to shares and underwrite public issues. SICOM also offers term loan, bridging loan and trouble shooting loan in deserving cases.

As of March 1986, SICOM has assisted 2091 units under package scheme of incentives, 148 units under MIDC incentives, 98 units under seed capital scheme. Total units assisted by SICOM was 4360 in March 1986.

MSSIDC

MSSIDC renders various types of assistance to small scale industries. These assistance include marketing of products, supply of raw materials, warehousing facilities, import and export assistance etc. MSSIDC markets the products of SSI units to the Government and semi-government organisations under its contract marketing scheme. It also produces and distributes raw materials to SSI units at the door step of industries. MSSIDC has developed warehousing facilities for the small scale industries while it provides import assistance for the raw materials not available in the country it also provides assistance to SSI units to export their products. MSSIDC, as can be seen from the above, is providing many crucial services to SSI units in the State.

Regional Development Corporation

Regional level corporations also play very important role in promoting industries and entrepreneurship in the state. Their main objectives are to promote local entrepreneurship and to develop local resource based industries. The major functions of such corporations are :

(a) Promotional and Development Services for the entrepreneurs, and
(b) Starting industrial projects of its own or in participation.

In order to perform the above function, they coordinate the activities of various state level organisations in the region and guide the new entrepreneurs. They also implement the Government scheme of incentives, build the mini industrial areas, provide incentives to educated unemployed, assist the ancilliary industries in developing and marketing their products.

State Incentives

The State Government has devised its own scheme of incentives to encourage entrepreneurs to start industries in the State particularly in the backward and developing regions.

According to the modified scheme of incentives introduced in 1983 (and to be in force till 1988), the entire state has been classified into 4 categories viz., A B C & D, Group 'A' consist of the highly developed metropolitan areas of Bombay and Pune where no subsidy is available. Remaining areas of the state has been classified into B C & D regions, according to the level of development and graded subsidies are available to the industries in these regions. SICOM has been appointed as the implementing agency for the State Government The important subsidies in the Package Scheme - 1983 are:

(a) MIDC Incentives: Industrial units coming up in MIDC areas, Government/Cooperative industrial estates are eligible for an additional incentives at the rate of 5% of fixed assets subject to maximum Rs 5 lacs.

(b) Sales Tax Exemption (Part -I): A new industrial unit coming up in backward area will not be required to pay sales tax from 3 years to 5 years.

(c) Sales Tax Loan (Part II): The existing units which will set up new units in developing areas are eligible for interest free unsecured sales tax loan.

(d) Special Capital Incentives: Special capital incentives are available to all industrial units set up in B, C, D regions which will take the benefits under b above.

(e) Incentives for Expansion: Incentives are also available for the existing units for expansion and diversification.

(f) Pioneer Units: An important feature of package scheme of incentives is the liberal assistance for the pioneer units—a large scale unit coming up as the very first unit in any taluka with fixed assets of Rs 5 crores in 'C' areas (outside MIDC areas), and over Rs 2 crores in 'D' areas.

A pioneer unit claiming Part-I incentives will not be required to pay sales tax for a period of 9 years from commencement of production plus capital incentive at 20% of fixed assets with ceiling of Rs 40 lacs.

The brief discussion, as above, indicate that the State of Maharashtra has designed various types of incentives to suit the needs of different types of entrepreneurs and industries, to reach its goal of industrial dispersal and industrial promotion. U.P. has also introduced a number of incentives to promote industries in the state. There may not be much difference in quantum and range of subsidies in U.P. and Maharashtra. However, this author has noted a definite difference in the quality of service provided by the state agencies. Maharashtra has definitely an edge over the U.P., so far as the quality of service and implementation of incentives are concerned, we have arrived at this conclusion through field interview with entrepreneurs in Maharashtra and U.P. The entrepreneurs, particularly the first generation entrepreneurs in Maharashtra are more satisfied than their counterpart in U.P.

REFERENCES

1. R. Mukherjee, 'Business Pioneers of West', Business Standard, July 3, 1986.
2. Ramesh Dutt, 'The Economic History of India', The Publications Division, Ministry of Information & Broadcasting, Government of India, New Delhi (1960).
3. E. Stalley and R. Morse, 'Modern Small Industries for Developing Countries', McGraw Hills N.Y., 1965.
4. S.M. Palia, 'Managerial Training and Extension Services for Small Scale Industries' - Indian Experience in Development News (Vol. 4, 1984), IDBI, Bombay.
5. V.G. Patel, Innovations in Banking - The Gujarat Experiment, IDBI, Bombay, 1981.
6. V.G. Patel, op. cit.

Note:-

1. Statistical Information in Section B based on various issues of the Annual Reports, Brochures and other Publications of IDBI, IFCI, ICICI, GIDC, GIIC, UPICON Kanpur IED Lucknow GIIC Gujarat, etc.
2. Statistical Information in Section Ca based on publications of UPSIDC (Kanpur), PICUP (Lucknow), UPFC (Kanpur), UPSIC (Kanpur), Directorate of Industries, Government of U.P., Kanpur.
3. Statistical information in Section Cb based on the Publications of MIDC, MSFC, MSSIDC, SICOM (Bombay), Directorate of Industries, Government of Maharashtra (Bombay).

FIRST GENERATION ENTREPRENEURS : A FIELD STUDY

Objectives of Field Study

In the previous chapter, we have discussed about the process of industrial growth and entrepreneurship promotion in India during pre and post Independent period. During Post-Independent period the Government has made several attempts through various agencies to promote entrepreneurship in order to achieve sustained rate of industrial growth. After independence, the primary concern of the Government was to develop less developed/backward regions of the country. Special attention has been given to develop small scale industries and new entrepreneurs. We have already discussed about the various schemes that have been introduced by the Government to promote entrepreneurship particularly in backward regions.

As a result of various promotional measures, a large No. of new industrial units particularly in small scale sector have been established by the new entrepreneurs. These new entrepreneurs, who have first time taken entrepreneurship may be called 'First Generation Entrepreneurs'. These entrepreneurs have come with diverse social & economic background. We have made attempt to examine Socio-economic background, mobility and growth of the emerging first generation entrepreneurs through field study. The major objectives of our field study can be listed as following:

1. To study the background of the entrepreneurs in terms of age, qualification, experience etc.
2. To study the type of industries, size of investment and employment.
3. To study the motivating factors and the extent of mobility (social and geographical).
4. Role of financial institution in the process of entrepreneurship development.

5. Entrepreneurial contribution in terms of creation of investment and employment.

Methodology: We have collected the necessary data by using the popular technique known as 'Survey-Interview' method. A structured questionnaire for this purpose was constructed by keeping all relevant factors in mind. The questionnaire was administered to the industrial units selected through stratified sampling method. Attempt was made to collect the data from maximum No. of units in developed and backward regions from developed and less developed states. We have, selected Maharashtra (the most developed state in India) and Uttar Pradesh (a relatively backward state in India). We have selected 2 districts in Maharashtra, Aurangabad '(a notified backward district) and Ahmadnagar, (a non-backward district but identified as a developing district). In U.P., we have selected 6 districts, out of which Kanpur Dehat, Unnao and Bulandshahr are backward districts while Aligarh, Kanpur and Mirzapur are non-backward Districts most developed State in India) and Uttar Pradesh (a relatively backward state in India). We have selected 2 districts in Maharashtra, Aurangabad (a notified backward district) and Ahmadnagar, (a non-backward district), In U.P. we have selected 6 districts, out of which Kanpur Dehat, Unnao and Bulandshahr are backward districts, while Aligarh, Kanpur and Mirzapur are non backward districts.

Location, Type and Size of Units

Location : Our sample data was collected from the industrial units located in Government Cooperative and private industrial areas. In spite of frequent visits and best efforts we could collect 106 questionnaire out of which 6 were rejected because they did not contain full information. Out of remaining 100 questionnaires statewise and areawise distribution of the units are shown in Table 4.1

Table 4. 1 : Areawise Distribution of Industrial Units

State	AREA Backward (i)	Non-backward (ii)	Total (i + ii)
U.P	36	29	65
Maharashtra	25	10	35
Total	61	39	100

It can be observed from the above that out of 100 units, 65 i.e 65% units are located in U.P and 35 i.e. 35% units are located in Maharashtra. Out of 100 units, 61% of the units are located in backward districts and 39 units are located in non-backward districts.

Further classification of sample units according to industrial area/complex has been made in Table 4.2.

Table 4.2 : Location of Sample Units

Serial No.	Name of the area	District	State	Status	No. of units
(i)	(ii)	(iii)	(iv)	(v)	(vi)
1.	Unnao	Unnao	U.P.	Backward	16
2.	Rania	Kanpur (Dehat)	U.P.	Backward	6
3.	Khurja	Bulandshahr	U.P.	Backward	14
4.	Aligarh	Aligarh	U.P.	Non-Backward	9
5.	Panki	Kanpur	U.P.	Non-Backward	15
6.	Mirzapur	Mirzapur	U.P.	Non-Backward	5
7.	Chikalthan	Aurangabad	Maharashtra	Backward	14
8.	Aurangabad	Aurangabad	Maharashtra	Backward	11
9.	Ahmadnagar	Ahmadnagar	- do -	Non - Backward	10
	Total No. of Units		-	--	100

Type of Organisation : Distribution of sample units, according to the type of Organisation in Table 4.3 indicate that out of 100, 55% was Proprietory units, 27% partnership and 18% private limited. While 33% of proprietory units were located in backward districts; 22% of such units were located in non-backward.

Table 4.3 : Organisation Type of Sample Units

	Type	U.P Backward	U.P Non-backward	Maharashtra Backward	Maharashtra Non-backward	Total Backward	Total Non-backward
	(1)	(2)	(3)	(4)	(5)	(6)	(7)
1.	Proprietory	21	18	12	4	33	22
2.	Partnership	7	8	7	5	14	13
3.	Private Ltd.	8	3	6	1	14	4
4.	Public Ltd.	-	-	-	-	-	-
	Total	36	29	25	10	61	39

There is 27% partnership units—more or less are equally distributed in backward and non-backward districts. However, out of 18 private limited units, 14 are located in backward districts. Usually the size of investment is higher in such units and the availability of incentives prompted such units in backward districts.

Size of the Units : The sample units have been distributed according to the size of Capital (Project costs) and employment.

The data in the Table 4.4 show that 60% of the units were having project cost upto Rs. 5 lakhs. There are 9% units having Project cost over Rs. 20 lakhs. It can be noted that there are 24 units, having uninvestment of more than Rs. 10 lakhs. Out of these, 10 were in non-backward and 14 in backward districts. Average size capital of the units (in backward as well as in non-backward districts) in Maharashtra was higher than that in U.P. However, the overwhelming majority of the units promoted by the first generation entrepreneurs are small in terms of capital investment.

Table 4.4: Frequency Distribution of Sample Units according to Size of Project Costs

Rs. in lakhs

Size	No. of Units U.P. B	NB	Maharashtra B	NB	Total B	NB	Grand Total (B+NB)
Upto 5	27	17	12	4	39	21	60
Over 5 to 10	5	7	3	1	8	8	16
Over 10 to 20	1	4	9	1	10	5	15
Over 20	3	1	1	4	4	5	9
Total	36	29	25	10	61	39	100

B = Backward Areas —   NB = Non Backward Areas

Average employment in Sample units is also small. There are 40 units having employment upto 10 persons and only 7 units having employment of more than 100 persons. Out of these 7, 6 are in non-backward districts and 1 in a backward district. Again, out of the above 7, 6 are in Maharashtra— 5 being in non-backward districts and 1 in backward district. The data also indicate that average employment is less in the units in backward districts than that in non-backward districts. Further, the average employment is relatively low in U.P. than in Maharashtra.

First Generation Entrepreneurship: A Field Study

Table 4.5 : Frequency Distribution of Sample Units according to Size of Employment

Size of employment No	U. P. B	U. P. NB	Maharashtra B	Maharashtra NB	Units B	Grand Total NB	(B+NB)
Upto 10	18	15	7	Nil	25	15	40
Over 10 to 25	13	8	3	2	16	10	26
Over 25 to 50	5	5	8	2	13	7	20
Over 50 to 100	Nil	Nil	6	1	6	1	7
Over 100	Nil	1	1	5	1	6	7
Total	36	29	25	10	61	39	100

B = Backward   NB = Non-backward.

Entrepreneurs : Age, Qualification and Experience

Though there are 100 units in our sample, the No. of entrepreneurs taken to study are 122. It is because, we have considered all the partners of partnership units separately for the purpose of discussing age, qualifications, background etc. In case of Private Ltd Units, the background of Promoters have been considered. Out of total 122 entrepreneurs, 80 are from U.P. and 42 from Maharashtra. Out of 122, 74 are from backward districts and 48 are from non-backward districts.

Age: Age factor of the new entrepreneurs is very important in a developing economy. Because, age of entrepreneur 'acts' as a critical factor in self development and the growth of the organisation. Young people, due to their exposure to latest science, technology and management are expected to introduce innovation in trade and industry. They also do not follow conservative business approach and bring more dynamism in industrial development and economic growth. The data in the Table 4.6 shows that 72 entrepreneurs are below 41 years of age.

Out of 72 entrepreneur 69% are in backward regions and 31% are in non-backward regions. It is also evident that the percentage of entrepreneurs over 41 are more in non-backward regions. There were 26 such entrepreneurs (out of 48) in backward regions while there were 24 such entrepreneurs in (out of 74) in backward regions.

Therefore, the percentage of entrepreneurs at higher age was 54% in non-backward regions and 32.4% in backward regions. The first generation entrepreneurs in Maharashtra belong to comparatively younger age group than that in U.P. and the more entrepreneurs are younger in backward regions.

Table 4.6 : Age Composition of Entrepreneurs

Age Group	U. P. B	U. P. NB	Maharashtra B	Maharashtra NB	Total Units B	Total Units NB	Total (B+NB)
(1)	(2)	(3)	(4)	(5)	(6)	(7)	(8)
							(6+7)
20-30	12	5	8	1	20	6	26
31-40	16	15	14	1	30	16	46
41-50	10	14	9	6	19	20	39
51 & Above	4	4	1	2	5	6	11
Total	42	38	32	10	74	48	122

B = Backward   NB = Non-backward

Education: One of the important precondition of industrialisation and economic development is the availability and induction of technology in various sectors. Induction and use of technology require skilled and competent managers and entrepreneurs. The skill and competence can be acquired through education and training. Entrepreneurs in addition to the above have to perform some other functions. According to S.R.Harris, "Perception of opportunities, gaining control over resources and managing in going enterprises are primary functions of entrepreneurship, regardless of the individual's willingness to undertake entrepreneurial activities. These desires will not be realised if the necessary capacity to carry them out is lacking. Education, occupational experience and access to technical information should each play a crucial role".[1]

Education, of course, is not a deciding factor for entrepreneurial success but it is an important factor influencing significantly the efficiency and success of entrepreneurs. Modern entrepreneurs are risk bearer and innovators which call for command over technology. Education gives an access to modern technology, which is very essential in the modern industry. Education also gives

First Generation Entrepreneurship: A Field Study

an exposure to outside world. Therefore, in a rapidly changing environment illiterate and untrained entrepreneurs will not be able to compete successfully. Education also helps as a contact factor to the new entrepreneurs without much social base and resources education has, therefore, been treated as a very important success factor of entrepreneurs.

In view of the importance of education, we have made an analysis of the educational background of the first generation entrepreneurs (Table 4.7) It can be observed that out of 122 entrepreneurs, only 4 are below SSC, 16 are Intermediates, 12 are Diploma-holders, 56 are Graduates and 29 are Post Graduates in different disciplines.

Table 4.7 : Educational Qualification of Entrepreneurs

	Qualification	U. P. B	U. P. NB	Maharashtra B	Maharashtra NB	Total B	Total NB	Total
	(1)	(2)	(3)	(4)	(5)	(6)	(7)	(6+7)
1.	Below SSC	2	-	1	1	3	1	4
2.	SSC & Intermediate	8	4	2	2	10	6	16
3.	Graduates (General)	18	8	3	3	21	11	32
4.	Post Graduate (General)	5	10	8	1	13	11	24
5.	Diploma (Tech)	4	2	6	0	10	2	12
6.	Graduate (Tech)	3	10	9	2	12	12	24
7.	Post Graduate (Tech)	1	2	2	-	3	2	5
8.	Others	1	2	1	1	2	3	5
	Grand Total	42	38	32	10	74	48	122

Notes : (1) Graduate and Post Grauuates in General category includes those who obtained degrees in" Arts, Science and Commerce.

(2) Diploma holder, Graduates and Post Graduates in Technical discipline includes Engineers, technicians, etc.

In our sample of 122 entrepreneurs, there are 45.9% graduates and 23.8% Post Graduates. (General & Technical). About 30% of entrepreneurs are Graduates & Post Graduates in Engineering and

Technology. This percentage is very significant in view of the General rate of literacy and growth of technical education. In 1981, the general rate of literacy was 36%. As per University Grants Commission Report[2] (1981-82), the percentage of student enrolment (in College and Universities) in the Faculty of Engg. & Technology was only 4.4% The percentage of Post Graduate students in the same year (in all faculties) was 9.7%. Therefore, the educational background of entrepreneurs in our sample is very encouraging. Statewise distribution indicate that in U.P. 57, out of 80 were Graduates and Post Graduate (i.e. 71.3%), while in Maharashtra, this was 28 (out of 42) i.e. 66. 7%. However, the percentage of Engineer and Technologist entrepreneurs was higher in Maharashtra (45.2%) than in U.P. (27.5%) probably due to higher rate of literacy and growth of technical education in Maharashtra.

Experience: Like education and training, experience also plays an important role in improving efficiency in management, production and control. Personal experience of entrepreneurs, particularly, for small scale entrepreneurs are very important, because they have to perform several functions to mobilise resources, direct and control production, supervise marketing/sales and render (if necessary) after sales-service. Therefore, post experience in some areas will definitely put him in advantageous position and would reduce his dependence on hired employees. It is always better to have some experience because experienced person will always have an edge over the inexperienced person in any field.

Experience of the entrepreneurs in our sample has been classified into 3 categories, namely, experience in 'same line', 'in other line' and 'no experience'. Among the unexperienced most of them were unemployed before starting industries, some, however, had received some training either in the same or in any different discipline. We can see from the data in the Table 4.8 that 40 i.e. 32.8% had experience in the same line, 49 i.e. 40.2% and 33 i.e. 27% were not having any experience before starting the unit.

The data also indicate that more person without and with experience in the same line started industries NB districts, and more persons with experience in other line started industries in backward districts. This shows that the backward districts could attract persons with diverse experience.

First Generation Entrepreneurship: A Field Study

Table 4.8 : Past Experience of the Entrepreneurs

Experience	U.P. (U) B	U.P. (U) NB	Maharashtra (M) B	Maharashtra (M) NB	Total (U+M) B	Total (U+M) NB	(6+7)
(1)	(2)	(3)	(4)	(5)	(6)	(7)	(8)
1. Same	10	14	14	2	24	16	40
2. Other line	21	13	11	4	32	17	49
3. No experience	11	11	7	4	18	15	33
Total	42	38	32	10	74	48	122

Percentage analysis of (past) experience as done in Table 4.9 indicate an interesting trend. In our sample 27% entrepreneurs had no past experience, while about 40% had experience in other lines and about 32% in the same line. The data also indicate that there is a higher percentage of less experienced (in terms of years) entrepreneurs in U.P. and higher percentage of entrepreneurs with more experience in Maharashtra. Similarly, percentage of un-experienced persons are also more in U.P. This indicate that entrepreneurs from cross section of people and unemployed are attracted at higher rate in U.P. than in Maharashtra which is definitely a significant trend of entrepreneurship development in less developed states like U.P.

Table 4.9 : Length of Experience

Experience	U.P.	Maharashtra	Total
1. Same line	23.75	21.43	22.95
0. 10 yrs	6.25	16.67	9.84
2. Other line			
0-10 yrs	26.25	14.29	22.13
Over 10 yrs	16.25	21.42	18.03
3. No experience	27.50	26.19	27.05
	(100.00%)=80	(100.00%=42)	(100.00%=122)

But to what extent the experience has helped the entrepreneurs is a matter of further investigation. It has been noted from the interview that there is higher degree of confidence and stability among the entrepreneurs in Maharashtra than that in U.P. However, general industrial climate in Maharashtra is also a contributory factor to this confidence. However, the importance of education training and experience cannot be ignored. Following S. R. Harris, we can state "Education, occupational experience and access to technical information are such important in enabling an individual to perceive that potentially profitable opportunity that exists. Whether or not that perceived opportunity is actually exploited depend on the motivation of the individual and his ability to marshall the necessary resources."[3]

Motivation and Mobility of Entrepreneurs

Entrepreneurial Motivation

An entrepreneur is an agent who has to perform several functions to mobilise and utilise resources and to create market in order to earn maximum return. He ventures into an uncertain future to exploit the potentiality that exists. Entrepreneurship, therefore is a very risky proposition. He may swim, he may sink. Even knowing this, people accept it. In our field study, we have come across entrepreneurs who left very cosy jobs and started very small unit personally supervising all the works. We have come across petty businessmen who were doing well but put their hard earned money at stake. Technologists and Engineers (who are fresh from University) started industry instead of going for safe jobs. These people, who are called 'marginal men' certainly have something different in them. According to David Maclleland, these people have very high achievement motivation (n-achievement[4]). They are the achievement oriented people who want to take personal responsibility, tend to persist in the face of adversity, tend to take moderate risk, tend to know the results of their efforts. They are innovative, full of interpersonal competence and fight for the well accomplish long term goals. According to Meclleland, they are unusually creative, having high propensity of risk taking capacity and a strong need for achievement. The supply of entrepreneurs in a country depends on the No. of this type of people who are usually small in number. It has been shown by the researchers that there are 6 important need which lead a man to creative enterprise like entrepreneurship. These needs are achievement, recognition, work itself, responsibility, advancement and salary. Existence of these qualities (single or in combination) lead one to take up entrepreneurship, though that is risky.

First Generation Entrepreneurship: A Field Study

Table 4.10 : Factors Effecting Motivation of Entrepreneurs

Factor	U.P.(U) B	U.P.(U) NB	Maharashtra (M) B	Maharashtra (M) NB	Total (U+M) B	Total (U+M) NB	(6+7)
(1)	(2)	(3)	(4)	(5)	(6)	(7)	(8)
1. Income	12	10	8	2	20	12	32
2. Social Recognition	6	4	4	4	10	8	18
3. Independent/own work	8	7	8	2	16	9	25
4. Achievement/responsibility	3	4	3	1	6	5	11
5. Self advancement employment	10	8	3	0	13	8	21
6. More than one factor	2	3	4	1	6	4	10
Total	41	36	30	10	71	46	117

We have made an attempt to examine the above achievement factors in our study. We have asked the respondents to identify the motivating factor for starting their unity. Out of 122, we could get the response from 117 entrepreneurs. Out of 117, 10 have indicated more than one motivating factors. Distribution of the entrepreneurs, according to the primary motivating factors as assigned them has been shown in the Table 4.10. It can be noted that the highest No. of entrepreneur 32 (26.23%) were motivated by monetary consideration. Close observations have revealed that most of these entrepreneurs were traders/businessmen and few were salaried employees. Second most dominating factor was independent job. Twenty five (21.38%) entrepreneurs started industries due to their desire to have independent work or to do something of their own. Most of these entrepreneurs were former salaried employees who were not satisfied with the working environment, nature of job, style of management and opportunity for work.

Third important factor of motivation, as stated by the entrepreneurs, is self-advancement. However, out of 21, 16 were unemployed and the basic objective was to create some employment opportunity for them. The rest stated that they wanted self advancement i.e. to rise in the life. Social recognition or social status was also an important factor to draw the entreprenurs in the risky venture of manufacturing. Most of these people were businessmen and traders who earned money through business but could not get social recognition. Therefore, they intended to acquire social recognition by becoming entrepreneurs.

There were 11 entrepreneurs for whom the main driving force was achievement or to involve themselves in more responsible work. These entrepreneurs wanted to achieve something in life.

Most of the technologists and executive were engaged in work of creative and specialised nature. But the urge for achievement could not be fulfilled and they preferred to satisfy their urge for achievement through entrepreneruship.

There are only 10 entrepreneurs who clearly had sated that more than one factors have motivated them. However, it seems in case of a large No. of entrepreneurs motivation was due to several factors. Probably due to time factor i.e. decision to start the unit and our interview, the importance of certain factors had reduced.

We have also enquired about the assisting factors which influenced their primary motivation factors. Because, it is not only the desire to achieve (or need for achievement) but also the favourable existence of certain other factors which translated the desire into reality. From the data, we have observed that the above motivational factors were significantly influenced by certain assisting factors like family environment, (business family), technical knowledge (through educational or through past employment) training and Government incentives. Entrepreneurs from business family were having financial support, past employees had social contact, engineers were having technical competence. Therefore, it is difficult to single out any particular motivating factor. In spite of the limitation, we can say that the most important were 'Pull' factors that is income, social recognition etc. which acted very strongly to induce the entrepreneurs to start the industry. Moreover, most of the entrepreneurs were self motivated. Because very few in our sample received EDP training or were encouraged by others. Self motivation, however was influenced by the existence of certain favourable factors as mentioned earlier.

Entrepreneurial Mobility

Social Mobility

One of the important characteristics of an achievement oriented person is that he puts all his efforts to realise his goal. For achieving certain thing he does not mind to move geographically. He also attempts to move upward in the social ladder by breaking all the barriers-caste, community, profession or income, because the entrepreneurship offer tremendous opportunity for self advancement and social mobility. In the words of Mark Casson (5) 'even an economically disadvantaged person, who wish it to the top, may find it easier to do so through entrepreneurship than through other "means". But, in India, it has been evident that social mobility through entrepreneurship is still strongly influenced by the caste and family background. Because people with business background have better access to capital than the other. However, it has been observed that, of late, a sizeable No. of new entrepreneurs are coming from non business background particularly due to several scheme of incentives and promotional assistance. In this section, we have investigated the nature of social and regional mobility of entrepreneur in our sample.

Social mobility has been examined in terms of parental profession, though many may raise doubt about it. But we do not find any other easily acceptable method.

It is evident from the data (Table 4.11) that, in general, the highest percentage of entrepreneurs, that is 48.36% came from the family of traders and businessmen. Among others 33.6% came from the family which depended on service and 9% were from agriculturists' family.

Statewise position indicate that the representation of entrepreneurs from the family depending or service was about 33% in U.P. and 36% in Maharashtra. A striking difference is noted in case of traders/businessman's representation, which was 51.25% in U.P. against 42.9% in Maharashtra. The representation of agriculturist in our sample is very low probably due to the fact the agriculture still provides tax free income in India. However, it is interesting to note that a very large number of first generation entrepreneurs are from service background, where business and industry is controlled by the families of businessmen.

Table 4.11 : Family Background of Entrepreneurs

Profession	U.P.(U) B	U.P.(U) NB	Maharashtra(M) B	Maharashtra(M) NB	Total (U M) B	Total (U M) NB	Total (6+7)
(1)	(2)	(3)	(4)	(5)	(6)	(7)	(8)
1. Service	14	12	13	2	27	14	41
2. Trade & business	4	17	10	8	34	25	59
3. Agriculture	4	2	5	-	9	2	11
4. Professional	-	2	1	-	1	2	3
5. Other	-	5	3	-	3	5	8
	42	38	32	10	74	48	122

A similar observation was made by R.A. Sharma who says "of more importance is the entrepreneurial participation from non business background. The business and allied activities still constitute the dominant source of supply of entrepreneurial families but what is striking is that the individual promoters having their immediate background before branching out into industry as business executives, technicians, lawyers, Government servants and doctors are swelling the ranks of industrialists".[6] The emergence of this section of new entrepreneurs was brought attitudinal change by virtue of their better educational-technical knowledge etc. In fact structural change in Indian industry was significantly influenced by the emergence of this entrepreneurial class who are highly educated, innovative, enterprising and usually free from conservatism in business management.

However the most discouraging feature Indian entrepreneurship development is the poor representation of rural rich. In fact this is a contradiction to the Japanese development, where 'elite' and landed aristocracy (samurai) entered into industrial activities through entrepreneurship and put the Japan in the world industrial map. Takeo Tsuchiya wrote 'that in the case of Japan, the feudalistic samurai or their sons shouldered the leadership role of the Meiji entrepreneur. Unlike any other nation, the development of capitalism guided by bureaucrats who were samurai and by business leaders who were also of Samurai Origins"[7]

In India, rural rich are still shy about investing in industrial activities. Participation of this section people would reduce the problem of unproductive investment by rural rich and enhance the supply of financial capital for rural industrial investment. Those who are entering into industry with 'service' background usually depend on financial institutions for capital. It has been noted by this Author[8] that the average size of fixed capital of such type of entrepreneurs is very small comparing to that of units started by traders/businessmen. It is, therefore, necessary to find out the way to induce these rural rich to entre industry and channalise the idle rural resources for productive use.

Regional Mobility

Inter regional and intra regional mobility is an important characteristics of achievement oriented people. Like social barriers, they can break the geographical barriers. If opportunity and potentiality exist this type of entrepreneurs will move from their home town to that place.

Table 4.12 : Regional Mobility of Entrepreneurs

Original base of Entreprenuers	U.P. (U) B	NB	Maharashtra (M) B	NB	Total (U + M) B	NB	Total (6+7)
(1)	(2)	(3)	(4)	(5)	(6)	(7)	(8)
Local	25	27	10	3	35	30	65
Outsider	17	11	22	7	39	18	57
Total	42	38	32	10	74	48	122

Data in Table 4.12 indicate that out of 122, there are 57 outside entrepreneurs who have migrated from other regions/districts. In fact, this is very high number comparing to the Indian social condition where attachment of people with the own locality is very strong. The percentage of outside entrepreneurs is significantly higher in Maharashtra, than that in U.P. It is because of the existing industrial climate, potentiality and opportunity. People migrate to other place if sufficient opportunities are not prevalent at their own place and if the better opportunities are available at distant place. The major factor of mobility is the availability of incentives in backward districts. We have noted that people came from far away to setup industrial units at A'bad, Chakalthana, Unnao, Rania due to the availability of financial and other incentives. We have located many entrepreneurs at Khurja who came from other states because Khurja offers agglomeration advantage of Pottery industries. Similar industrial complex at Panki and Unnao attracted entrepreneurs from distant places due to availability of shed and the market (at Kanpur).

Therefore, if potentiality and facilities are created to a certain level to help entrepreneurs, there will be an automatic increase in supply of entrepreneurs. It is a fact that entrepreneurship is not only a product of motivation but also the favourable existence of social and economic factors, particularly the access to resources.

We have already noted that several agencies are involved in promoting entrepreneurship through motivational efforts—E.D.P. training and other financial and non-financial incentives. Financial institutions, in this respect, are playing very important role. In the next section an account of the role and assistance of financial institutions in promoting entrepreneurs has been furnished.

Role of Financial Institutions

One of the major constraints of entrepreneurship is the lack of access to capital. Even the potential entrepreneurs with very high achievement orientation will not be able to realise his goal if he has no access to resources. In India, resource constraint, particularly for the first generation entrepreneurs specially those who are from non-business community is very acute. Therefore, to solve this problem financial institutions have introduced several schemes of incentives like concessional finance (term loan, seed capital etc.) The central and State Governments also offer capital linked investment subsidy, industrial land and constructed sheds at cheaper rate. All these incentives induced the potential entrepreneurs to establish industrial units even at a distant places (from their home town/ District/ States).

Location, pre-requisites like market, transport, raw materials etc. are very important for location decision. McMillan Jr.[9] has noted that the plant location has no choice but to accept the region which provides the basic pre-requisites. However, the entrepreneur does have choice as to where to locate within the region. It is this choice which is constrained by determinants such as taxes, business and political climate, low price of land, room for further expansion etc. These pre-requisites or location factors can be classified into two categories, viz, Pull factors (like financial and non-financial incentives) and 'Push factors' (like location control). Interplay of these factors decide the location of particular industry. However, it has been observed by us that in India, 'Pullfactors'exert more influence on the location decision of small industries started by first generation entrepreneurs whereas 'Push factors' are important determinant of Plant location in Large Scale sector.[10]

Sample data revealed that the entrepreneurs had assigned most importance to the availability of financial incentives for deciding location. Out of 100 units 35% of 35 units had considered financial incentives as the primary factor to select the location of the Unit. Non-financial incentives had been considered as a primary factor by 25 units. Therefore, incentives together was the deciding factors for 60 units in our sample. It is also interesting to note that financial incentives were stronger in backward regions while the non-financial incentives were stronger in non-backward regions. Market, raw materials exerted relatively less influence on location decision of the sample units. However, other factors (which include nearness to home town) exerted third most important influence on location decision.

Incentives, particularly financial incentives exerted stronger influence in Maharashtra than in U.P. In Maharashtra, 21 units (out of total of 35) i.e. 60% units were primarily influenced by financial incentives. This percentage was 21.5% in U.P. This trend is probably due to the fact that implementation of the scheme in Maharashtra is better than that in U.P., and secondly, a large percentage of units in Maharashtra were pushed outside Bombay-Thane-Pune belt. The policy of industrial dispersal followed sincerely by Maharashtra Government which pushed many of the entrepreneurs outside Bombay/Pune industrial belt

Table 4.13 : Determinants of Location Decision

Location factors	U.P. B	U.P. NB	Maharashtra B	Maharashtra NB	Total B	Total NB	Total (6+7)
(1)	(2)	(3)	(4)	(5)	(6)	(7)	(8)
1. Financial incentives	12	2	17	4	29	6	35
2. Non-financial incentives	8	10	3	4	11	14	25
3. Nearness to market	5	4	3	-	8	4	12
4. Nearness to source of raw material	3	3	-	1	3	4	7
5. Other factor	8	10	2	1	10	11	21
Total	36	29	25	10	61	39	100

B = Backward   NB = Non Backward

This entrepreneurs, preferred to locate their units in such a locations where incentives are available with other facilities. Moreover, the 'location inertia' as seen from item No. 5 Table 4.13 is stronger in U.P. than in Maharashtra. Local entrepreneurs, instead of availing of incentives at far away places preferred to stay nearer home town. Finally, the industries located in Unnao, Rania, Panki, were nearer to Kanpur—the most industrialised city of North—which acted as a good market and raw material centres. These factors have marginally reduced the importance of incentives in U.P.

It is evident from the above discussion that the incentives, particularly financial incentives exerted significant influence, on location decision of first generation entrepreneurs.

The main reason behind this was the resource constraint of the small entrepreneurs. We have noted that a very high percentage of entrepreneurs in our sample are from non-business families. They had not much command over resources and had to depend on Government supply of resources (through subsidy, concessional finance etc). If we analyse the source of finance of the units, it will be evident that there is 'near total' dependence on Government agencies for finance.

We have collected information regarding the source of capital (project cost) at the time of starting the industrial units, which gives an indication of extent of dependence on the Government agencies for initial capital. It has been observed by us that in general, the units in backward regions received 70% to 90% of project costs from the Government agencies. Their own capital contribution was very small even in some cases it was 5% of total project cost. The rest was arranged from financial institutions, government, banks. However, the own contribution towards project cost was somewhat more in non-back-ward districts. Most of the units in our sample from Maharashtra received either central investment subsidy or State Government capital subsidy. Lesser No. of units in U.P. sample received investment subsidies.

In spite of limitation of data, it is evident that the financial institutions had played a very crucial role by supplying necessary financial resources to these entrepreneurs. Therefore, it can safely be said on the basis of the statistical information that majority of the first generation entrepreneurs could not start their own projects in absence of financial support from the financial institutions and the backward regions would have lost the investment and employment generated by these industrial units.

Entrepreneurail Contribution to Investment and Employment

The ultimate objectives of the schemes of incentives and the efforts to promote entrepreneurship are to attract industrial investment in the less developed/backward regions to generate employment and income. It is, therefore, necessary to examine the extent of investment and employment created by the sample units.

The data in Table 4.14 indicate that out of 100 units, 61 units are in backward regions and 39 units are in non-backward regions. The total project cost (fixed capital in land building and machinery) of these units estimated at 1062 lakhs and they have created direct employment for 3198 persons. Investment in backward and non-backward regions was Rs. 575 lakhs and Rs. 487 lakhs respectively. Employment in backward and non-backward regions were 1556 and 1642 respectively. Average fixed capital and employment in our sample was Rs. 10.62 lakhs and Rs. 32.0 persons per unit while the average capital per employment was Rs. 0.33 lakhs.

Table 4.14: Areawise Distribution of Investment and Employment in Sample Units

Region/ industrial area	Total No. of units	Total project cost (Rs. lakhs)	Total employment (No.)	Average project cost (Rs. lakhs)	Average employment (No.)	Capital per employment (Rs. lakhs)
(1)	(2)	(3)	(4)	(5)	(6)	(7)
A. Backward Areas						
1. Chikathana	15	185	782	12.33	52.13	0.24
2. A'bad	10	71	272	7.10	27.20	0.26
3. Unnao	15	113	206	7.53	13.73	0.55
4. Rania	6	176	95	29.33	15.83	1.85
5. Khurja	15	30	201	2.0	13.40	0.15
Total (A)	61	575	1556	9.4	25.5	0.37
B. Non-Backward Areas						
1. A'bagar	10	273	1149	27.3	114.9	0.24
2. Kanpur	15	94	176	6.3	11.7	0.53
3. Aligarh	10	110	280	11.0	28.0	0.39
4. Mirzapur	4	10	37	2.5	9.3	0.27
Total (B)	39	487	1642	12.5	42.1	0.30

Average project cost of the units in backward areas was Rs. 9.4 lakhs as against Rs. 12.5 lakhs in non-backward areas. Average employment per unit was 25.5 persons in backward regions as against 42 persons in non-backward areas and capital per unit of employment was Rs. 0.37 lakhs in backward areas as against 0.30 lakhs in non-backward areas.

Statewise bifurcation indicate that the investment and employment (in 35 units) in Maharashtra were Rs. 529 lakhs and 2203 persons respectively while the same in U.P. was Rs. 533 and 995. Therefore, average project cost was Rs. 15.11 lakhs in Maharashtra and 8.2 in U.P. per unit employment cost being Rs. 0.24 lakhs.

In U.P. the average project cost was Rs. 8.20 lakhs and average employment was 15.30 person and per unit employment cost was Rs. 0.53 lakhs. Therefore, there is an indication that in U.P. the units are in general smaller in terms of employment and investment than that in Maharashtra, but the per unit cost of employment is higher in U.P. than in Maharashtra. This fact reveals that capital intensity is more in industries in U.P. than in Maharashtra.

The data in the Table 4.14 indicate that average investment per unit was lower in backward areas than that in non-backward areas. However, the average employment was also lower in backward areas. This is due to the fact that there is a tendency among the entrepreneurs to promote capital intensive industries in backward areas, because of availability of central subsidy which depend on the capital investment.

Therefore, in order to achieve the desired result i.e. to create more employment opportunities through promotion of entrepreneurship and industrial development, efforts should be made to introduce employment subsidy instead of capital subsidy. However, in spite of the trend of growth of capital intensive industries in backward regions, the policy of incentives has been able to promote the entrepreneurs who have created employment opportunities particularly for local people.

In addition to creation of direct employment for 3198 persons, the activities of 100 units have also created indirect employment for many people. Of course, the indirect employment linkage is significantly directed outside the region and the better part of employment income multiplier will be felt outside the region. But if we consider the totality of impact in general, the gain is substantial. Therefore, it can be said that the policy of incentives and institutional efforts to promote new entrepreneurs have no doubt achieved significant success in realising the goal to create income and employment opportunities through promotion of new industries, particularly in small scale sector.

REFERENCES

1. Harris, S.R., 'Nigerian Entrepreneurship in Industry', in Growth and Development of Nigerian Economy (ed Carl Eicher and Carl Liedholm) Michigan State University Press, 1970.

2. University Grants Commission (Government of India) Reports for the year 1981-82 (Our source : Basic Statistics on Indian Economy 1984; Commerce Research Bureau, Bombay).

3. Harrish, J.R., I.B.I.D.

4. McCelleland, D.C. and Winter, D.G. et al. Motivating Economic Achievement, Free Press, New York, 1969.

5. Casson Mark, 'The Entrepreneurs—An Economic Theory' Moretin Robertson, Oxford, 1982.

6. Sharma, R.A., 'Entrepreneurial Change in Indian Industry', Sterling Publishers Ltd., New Delhi, 1980.

7. Tokeo Tsuchija, Rectur on Economic History of Modern Japan, Tokyo (1958).

8. Sadhak, H., 'Industrial Development in Backward Regions in India,' Chugh Publisher, Allahabad (1986).

9. McMillian Jr., 'Why Manufacturers Choose Location vs Determinants of Plant Location', Land Economics, Aug. 1965, p. 299.

10. Sadhak H., IBID, pp. 259-276.

5

PERFORMANCE OF FIRST GENERATION ENTREPRENEURS

Introduction

In the previous chapter (Chapter-4), we have discussed about the characteristics of emerging entrepreneurial class particularly in backward regions in the light of primary data collected by us. We have noted that these first generation entrepreneurs have come from different socio-economic strata. The socio-economic background exert significant influence the level of achievement motivation, access to resources, risk bearing capacity etc., which in turn influence the growth of the enterprises. Locational environment also exert considerable influence on the functioning of the industrial units. While the easily available market, resource, infrastructure help the growth of units. Short supply of such factors will restrict the growth. We have therefore intended to examine some of the selected units from our sample to see the various aspects like entrepreneurial motivation, location decisions, working of the units and the constraints of growth. For this purpose, we have carefully selected 10, out of 100 units in our sample.

Out of 10 selected units, 6 are located in backward districts/areas and 4 are located in non-backward districts. These units are promoted by entrepreneurs coming from the families of agriculturist, traders/businessmen, educationist, and professionals. There are technocrats, unemployed, professionals etc. There are local, non-local and non-resident entrepreneurs.

The entrepreneurs have confronted various types of problems— some are location related, some are decision related and some are general problems—experienced by all the new entrepreneurs irrespective of their age, experience, qualifications and social contact. In these case studies we have tried to look at these aspects from a close quarter. However, these cases cannot be called fully representative of the total picture. Yet they reveal interesting stories of success and important problems required to be handled with care and urgency to help the first generation entrepreneurs to grow and for healthy growth of industrial sector in rural/backward regions.

Units Located in Backward Areas

There are 6 cases from the backward regions viz.

1. An import substitute unit.
2. A market located unit.
3. A tied unit.
4. A foot loose unit.
5. A local resource based unit.
6. A location pushed unit.

CASE STUDY - 1: An Import Substitute Unit

The Entrepreneurs : This industrial unit has been promoted by 2 young entrepreneurs—one, a graduate in engineering and the other a diploma holder in engineering. At the time of starting this unit they were in mid 30's. None of their family members were ever engaged in business, trading or industries. However these two entrepreneurs worked in different engineering industries before starting this unit.

From the questionnaire and interview it has been noted that these two youngmen are achievement oriented who wanted to start their own industries though they had to encounter a lot of difficulties particularly due to lack of finance. But they could fulfil their desires to set up own unit due to the various assistance of the Government.

They had to take very great risk (financial, careers and family) to leave their jobs and to start industry because they are from the very ordinary middle class families. However, sheer determination and high self-motivation induced them to take such risks.

Location of the Unit : This unit has been located in a Government Industrial area in Aurangabad district a notified backward district (which was eligible for central subsidy and) concessional finance. This unit got a constructed industrial shed and formally established in 1973, and had started commercial production in 1974.

The decision to set up the unit at this location was taken in view of the availability of concessional finance, central subsidy and industrial shed. Another decision factor was the location of home town in the area. Growth of industries in the region which has created a good market for the products, was also a factor influencing location decision.

Capital, Employment etc. : This unit started with fixed capital of Rs. 7.5 lacs (cost of plant machinery and shed) which increased to Rs. 12.38 lacs in 1981-82. The unit received 75% of fixed capital from financial institutions at concessional rate, 15% as central subsidy. They themselves contributed only 10% of fixed capital.

The unit primarily manufactures such tapes, which are (used in industry) usually imported from Japan. They collect 85% of necessary raw materials from Bombay and rest from Poona. About 30% of the products are sold to the industries in the district, 30% goes to other districts of the state and 40% to other states.

This unit has employed 16 persons including technical, skilled and unskilled labour, all of whom were recruited locally.

Working Results : Commercial production was started in 1974 and since then the unit had progressed steadily. Utilisation of installed capacity as well as sales and profit increased steadily after a severe set back in the second and third year when these young entrepreneurs had to face most troubled priod in their lives. Shortage of working capital and lack of sufficient order made them frustrated. However, that miserable days have passed due to their hard work and strong desire to succeed. Turnover and profit of the unit increased steadily and they did not look back, while the capacity utilisation was 40% in 1974-75, the same increased to 80% in 1981. Sales of the unit had gone up from Rs. 1,12,000 in 1975-76 to Rs. 3,83,000 in 1981 and the net worth had also increased from Rs. 57,000 in 1975-76 to Rs. 1,48,000 in 1981. This unit received president's award for import substitutes in 1981. At present the unit is functioning satisfactorily.

Constraints : It has been reported by the promoters that irregular supply of raw materials and high turnover of labour affected the production. Also the cumbersome legal and procedural formalities created problems for these entrepreneurs. The rate of interest of the state level financial institutions is too burdensome for them. They were in the opinion of flexible moratorium period.

CASE STUDY - 2 : A Market Located Unit

The Entrepreneur : The entrepreneur who is around 50, is a post graduate in Physics. Before starting this unit to manufacture paper goods, he was a academician. He taught in various colleges for about 20 years. He was not having any trading or business experience. None of his family members were in business.

This entrepreneur was fed up with teaching and was looking for some independent job which could give him better opportunities to fulfil his creative urges. It seems from the interview and questionnaire that he was not much satisfied with his limited independence and income of a teacher though it gave him social respectability. He wanted to find an avenue for more income.

Opportunities came to him with the declaration of his home district as a backward district, eligible for central subsidy and concessional finance. He selected a local demand based products i.e. note-books, registers and other paper goods usually used in educational and non-educational institutions.

Location of the Unit : This is a SSI unit located in a Government industrial estate in Aurangabad. The unit established in 1975. Land was available at concessional rate from the Government The location decision was taken in view of the following factors :

1. Readily available market for the products.
2. Availability of finance at concessional rate and eligibility for investment subsidy.
3. Readily available industrial shed.
4. Home town.

Capital, Employment etc. : The data in the questionnaire revealed that the initial project cost was Rs. 9.5 lacs (which increased to Rs. 12.00 lacs in 1981) out of Rs. 9.5 lacs the promoter contributed 16% and 69% was received from State Financial Corporation and the rest 15% as Central Investment Subsidy.

The unit employed 66 persons including 11 managerial personnels. All the employees were recruited locally. Therefore there was a strong local employment linkage.

The unit collects necessary raw materials from Bombay and Pune and naturally has to maintain a large inventory.

The units sold 50% of its products in the district and remaining 50% in the neighbouring districts of the region.

Working Results : The unit's operating results is quite satisfactory. Since inception the unit did not face any major problems except occasional problems regarding working capital. Capacity utilisation increased from 40% in 1975-76 to 75% in 1980-81. Turnover of the unit increased steadily. From net sales of Rs. 12 lacs in 1978-79 it had increased to 33 lacs in 1980-81. The entrepreneur was quite satisfied with the progress of the unit.

Constraints : The major constraints, as the entrepreneur reported, was rigid rules and regulations of financial and development institutions, which he felt, needs relaxation particularly for new entrepreneurs. More co-operation is required from Government officials for the better growth of industry in backward areas.

It has also been suggested that a single window service as well, as the arrangement for the working capital facilities from term lending institutions would reduce unnecessary burden and time lag for arranging working capital.

CASE STUDY - 3 : A Tied Unit

The Entrepreneur : The entrepreneur is in his mid 50 was well established engineer in a reputed firm in Calcutta. He is having 30 years experience as mechanical engineer. Though he was having technical experience he was not having any previous experience to handle business or trading. In 1977, he came across an advertisement of U.P. Government offering facilities to new industries in backward areas and offer of marketing tie up at a particular location. He became interested in that advertisement and contacted U.P. Government Department. His intention to start industry was due to his desire to set up his own manufacturing unit as well as to have same source of income after retirement. Therefore, to have continuous flow of income and gain more social status, the entrepreneur left his job and came to U.P. to start this unit at the age of 50.

Location of the Unit : This unit was established in early 1977 in an industrial complex of a backward district (in Uttar Pradesh) eligible for Central Government subsidy and concessional finance. The unit was located here due to :

1. Availability of shed in industrial complex.
2. Availability of concessional finance and subsidy.
3. Special tie up arrangement for the units (in this complex) with the U.P. Government.
4. Being nearer to Kanpur (the largest industrial city not only of U.P. but also of Northern India).

The unit started commercial production at the end of 1977. The important items of the unit to start with were, King pins, Shock pins etc., usually used in automobiles.

Capital, Employment etc. : The initial fixed capital excluding industrial shed was Rs. 2.5 lacs. The unit had received loans from UPFC and UPSIDC at concessional rate.

Initially the unit employed 10 skilled and unskilled worker. Out of which 4 were local and 6 outsiders. However, since 1980 only 4 workers are working (3 unskilled and 1 skilled).

It collects 100% raw materials from Kanpur—which is 60 km from the location of unit.

At present the unit is only doing job work. About 70% jobs are received from Kanpur and another 30% from this area. The entrepreneur now is surviving on job works only.

Working Results : The unit started production in 1977. In the first year i.e. 1977 sales of the unit was about Rs. 25,000 which increased to Rs. 1,73,000 in 1978. It has been informed by the entrepreneur that unit was established with an understanding that the State Government would purchase its products. However, later on the State Government backed out, the unit was also not able to establish in outside market due to shortage of capital. As a result, the unit switched over to job working in 1979. In 1985-86, there were only 4 workers and the total sales was Rs. 50,000 only. Though the unit started with high ambition, it could not be fulfilled specially because of marketing problem.

Constraints : The problem that has been experienced by the entrepreneur can be listed below :

1. The State Government did not keep its assurance and understanding to purchase its products. Therefore, 'marketing' became the major problem which could not be tackled. There is no other Government agency to help him in marketing products.
2. The unit did not receive necessary working capital from banks.
3. Though the unit located in an industrial complex situated in an industrial area, no infrastructure other than sheds and roads is available. There is no bank, post-office, shops and transport.
4. The entrepreneur also felt bitterly about the various Government Department, Co-ordinating Industrial Promotion activities.

5. The entrepreneur also felt that the selection of location was wrong. There is no local market. Government should not have encouraged the entrepreneurs to establish such type of industries at this location.

CASE STUDY - 4 : A Footloose Unit

The Entrepreneur : Our entrepreneur is a 32 years old automobile Diploma Engineer. His family had never any links to industry or business. Usually depends on service, though they have agricultural land. He was neither interested in agriculture nor in business.

After completing diploma course he was searching a job for more than a year but did not succeed. He then thought to start an industry. Though he was an automobile engineer he switched over to Chemical Industry due to its demand in the state market.

Location of the Unit : This unit is located at the Government Industrial Area in a backward district (in U.P.) which is eligible for Central subsidy and concessional finance. The important factors influencing location decision of the unit were :

(a) Availability of concessional finance and central subsidy.
(b) Cheaper Land.
(c) Other benefits like tax rebate.

Capital, Employment etc. : The unit has started in 1981 with fixed capital of Rs. 4.75 lacs, out of which about 20% was the contribution of the promoter. The rest was received from U.P.F.C. and U.P.S.I.D.C. The promoters contribution to working capital was 25% to 35%.

The unit has employed 16 persons out of which 3 are skilled, 9 are unskilled, and 4 are managerial personnels. Twelve were recruited locally and 4 from outside the district.

This unit require sulpher powder to manufacture sulpher roll. It collects the entire raw materials from outside. The supply is irregular and a large inventory is required to be maintained.

Working Results : The unit started commercial production in 1982. It collects its major raw materials from MMTC. It sold 50% of its product in U.P., the rest in Delhi.

The financial data indicate that the unit reached break even in 1982. There has been a steady increase in use of installed capacity, sales and profit and has taken a proposal for diversifying its activities.

Total sales of the unit increased from Rs. 1 lacs in 1982 to more than 22 lacs in 1986. The unit is progressing satisfactorily except some occasional setbacks. This unit has diversified in the related field.

Constraints : The unit has complaint about the severe infrastructural communication and transportation problems which are coming in the way of faster growth of the unit. They had also to face the problem of raw material (supply is irregular and the quantity is insufficient). One of the major complaints of the entrepreneur was the lack of enthusiastic guidance and assistance from the policy implementing authority. During the interview the entrepreneur said that the several schemes of incentives announced by the Government were not being implemented properly. He therefore felt that simplification of existing procedural formalities are necessary to help the genuine and deserving cases of new entrepreneurs.

CASE STUDY - 5 : A Resource Based Unit

The Entrepreneur : The promoter (entrepreneur) of the unit, (at the time of starting this unit) was around 50. He is a famous food technologist who served in many reputed food industries before establishing this unit. He had 30 years experience as a reputed food technologist. His family hails from a city in Maharashtra. The source of income of this middle class family is 'service'. The major motivating factor was to have his own enterprise, where he can put his own ideas and experience without any hindrance. It became evident from' our interview with the entrepreneur that he was rather interested to have something own to keep himself busy after his normal retirement. He did not seem to have very high-n ach, but an ordinary, entrepreneur not much of risk bearing mentality.

Location of the Unit : The unit has been located in a backward district in Maharashtra, quite far away from his home town. The important factors influencing the location decision were: locally available raw materials and Governments incentives. The unit was established in 1970 and commercial production started in the same year. The unit manufacture cereal and products.

Capital, Employment etc. : The total project cost of the unit was Rs. 2.4 lacs out of which about 20% was his own contribution, the rest was received as subsidy, loan from SICOM and commercial banks.

The unit employed 4 persons out of which 2 are skilled and 2 unskilled. All 4 were recruited locally and therefore, there is a strong employment linkage directed locally. But this is particularly in respect of unskilled and skilled labour. The managerial work is done by the entrepreneur himself and he is settled outside the region. Therefore, the impact of income multiplier is felt outside the region.

This unit collects about 95% of the required raw materials from the area of its location. Only 5% raw materials brought from other districts. This unit manufacture consumer goods which have very good market in the region. About 60% of the products are sold in the regional market and the rest 40% goes outside the region (which increased the transportation cost and the price of products).

Working Results : The performance of the unit as seen from the data provided by the entrepreneur, is not very satisfactory. The unit could not use more than 40% of its installed capacity. Total turnover of the unit remained more or less same during the last 3 years, and the unit was making constant losses and declared as a 'sick unit'.

Constraints : The major constraints of growth are (i) fluctuating price and irregular supply of raw materials, (ii) credit constraints, and (iii) lack of marketing facilities (due to shortage of working capital, the unit could not keep necessary inventory). It did not get necessary raw materials from any Government agency. Therefore, shortage of raw material was one of the major problems, though the unit was located here in view of availability of raw materials. Being a new unit it could not develop the necessary marketing channels. Therefore, though the product has good market it could not exploit it. Since the entrepreneur (promoter) is staying away from the factory and does not attend day to day activities of the unit, there is lack of proper supervision. Therefore in spite of the good potentiality, the unit became sick.

CASE STUDY - 6 : A Unit Pushed by Government Location Policy

Entrepreneur : The entrepreneur (promoter), who is in his mid 40's is a former technocrat of a reputed industrial organisation. Before starting this unit he worked for about 20 years as senior engineer in the same field. His father was a consultant and they have their own consultancy firm. Apart from consultancy their family was not having any link to any business/trading activities.

The immediate motivation came from his family environment. His long association with industries and success in consultancy induced him to start this unit. However, the data indicate that it was neither money nor employment but the respectability and social status of industrialist prompted him to start his own industrial unit.

Location of the Unit : The unit is located in a notified backward districts of Maharashtra. The district is eligible for concessional finance and Central Government subsidy. The unit is located at the Government industrial area. The location decision of the promoter was influenced by the :

1. Maharashtra Government's location policy.
2. Availability of concessional finance.
3. Availability of land.
4. Availability of cheap labour.

This private limited company was registered under DGTD and Factory Act in 1977. They were initially interested to locate this unit at Poona. But could not obtain N.O.C. (No Objection Certificate) and were bound to select an area outside Poona. Since they were to go out of Poona, the best course for them was to select an area eligible for incentives which not only offer all types of incentives but also a reasonable degree of infrastructural facilities.

Capital, Employment etc. : Capital structure of the unit indicate that the unit started with initial project cost of Rs. 35 lacs out of which 20% was contributed by the promoter, 70% by the state level financial institutions and 10% was received as Central Government investment subsidy. It was reported that the unit received very wonderful co-operation from state level institutions in respect of financial assistance.

This unit has employed 242 persons out of which 135 are employed in factory and 107 are at head office at Poona. Out of 12 managerial posts 10 are located at head office at Poona and 2 at factory (at A'bad). Out of 45 supervisory posts 20 are held by outsiders. There were 120 unskilled labours and all were recruited locally. It is therefore obvious that almost all the high salary jobs are held by the outsiders and a strong effect of income multiplier is felt outside the region.

So far the input output is concerned, it is also mainly directed outside the region. This unit imports 15% of its required raw material. It gets 80% from other states and 5% from Bombay.

The Unit is engaged in manufacturing—Coal fired bio-mess boilers for which there is a very good demand in India. About 10%

of the products are sold in the state while 90% of the products are sold in the other states in India.

Operating Results : Operating results indicated a steady progress of the unit. Turnover and profit had increased at a good space. Utilisation of installed productive capacity increased from 25% in 1977-78 to 80% in 1979-80 and it had further increased. While the unit sold boilers worth of Rs. 22 lacs in 1977-78, the same increased to 140 lacs in 1979-80.

Constraints : The major constraints reported by the entrepreneur are shortage of raw materials, labour unrest, labour turnover and lack of necessary infrastructural facilities in the area.

The unit has favour the relaxation of legal and procedural formalities imposed by the various financial and development agencies. Government should help the units in procuring raw materials. They also felt the usefulness of introducing employment subsidy for the new industries in the backward regions.

Units Located in Non-Backward Areas

In this section we have examined 4 industrial units established in non-backward districts/areas. The units have characteristic differences in respect of promoters, operating results and locational constraints. Background of the entrepreneurs also sharply differ from each other. While 2 entrepreneurs have considerable link to industries/business, and have easy access to financial resources, the 3rd unit was promoted by non-resident Indians and the 4th unit was promoted by an entrepreneur not having any significant access to financial resources or technology. These entrepreneurs have different story to tell about the progress of their units and problems that have experienced by them. The following 4 cases have been examined :

1. A connected unit.
2. A sick unit.
3. A traders unit.
4. A non-resident unit.

CASE STUDY - 7 : A Connected Unit

The Entrepreneur : The promoter (entrepreneur) of the unit is a technocraft (B.Tech.) who is 34 years old. Before starting his enterprise, he worked as an engineer in an engineering firm for 3 years, and gained practical experience. This young entrepreneur was not contended with his salary and the working environment. He therefore, wanted to start his own industry which would give him independence and more income.

Some of his relatives have industries and business, though his father was dependent on salaried employment. He was inspired by the success of his relations in industries and trading. Therefore, the major motivational factors were social/community influence, desire to earn more money and 'to be one's own master'. The entrepreneur had enough access to financial resources.

Location of the Unit : The unit was located in a Government industrial complex in non-backward district of Uttar Pradesh. This is a industrially developed area, where agglomeration advantages are available. The unit obtained an industrial shed and started production in 1977. The location decision was significantly influenced by the :

1. Location of Home Town.
2. Availability of industrial shed.
3. Readily available market for the products.
4. Other infrastructural facilities for the industries.

Capital, Employment etc. : This Private Ltd. firm started with initial fixed capital of Rs. 5 lacs which increased to Rs. 10 lacs in 1985-86. The promoter entrepreneur contributed 30% of fixed capital, the rest was taken as loans from banks. About 20% working capital was arranged by the promoter.

The total employment in the unit was 45 in 1985-86. There were 5 managerial, 20 skilled and 20 unskilled workers. Out of 45, 30 were local and 15 outsiders.

This unit manufactures electronic items for which it collects 30% raw materials from the local market and 70% from Delhi and other places.

About 25% of products are sold locally and 75% goes outside the state. It supplies to Government Department also.

Working Results : It seems from the data provided by the unit that the working result is quite satisfactory. In 1985-86, the unit could utilise 80% of installed capacity. Sales of the unit increased from Rs. 1.30 lacs in 1977 to Rs. 24.00 lacs in 1984-85.

This unit has diversified its activities and entered into consumer goods products in anticipation of growing competition for its products.

Constraints : This unit, like other units promoted first generation entrepreneurs had not experienced any serious problem of finance (fixed capital as well as working capital). However, they had the problems of raw materials (which is not available locally) and transportation. They have also experienced the marketing problem. In fact they could not succeed in pushing the products to the desired extent due to irregularity in transportation. Moreover, they do not get the necessary co-operation and assistance from the Government agencies. They also complaint about the non-existence of single window service, which would have solved the problems of time and saved the wasteful expenses.

CASE STUDY - 8 : A Sick Unit

The Entrepreneur : This is the story of an entrepreneur who was not having any inclination to enter into manufacturing activities but the circumstances forced him to do so. Our entrepreneur is a 42 years old science graduate who came from outside the state but settled down with his father. His entry was accidental. After graduation he was interested to pursue his study but his father forced him to enter into industry, to assist him. This unit was promoted by his father in 1970. Though initially he was not interested but after sometime he fully devoted himself and wanted to see that the unit grow and prosper. Therefore, it was not due to self motivation, but due to the circumstances that forced him to became an entrepreneur.

Location of the Unit : The unit is located in a co-operative industrial estate in a non-backward district of U.P. The family of entrepreneurs belong to other state but since they are settled in this area, they preferred to locate the unit there. Availability of market and industrial shed in the co-operative industrial were the determining factors. It is a proprietory firm started in 1970 to manufacture rubber goods.

Capital, Employment etc. : The initial project cost of the unit was Rs. 2 lacs. It had received more than 50% of fixed capital from banks. It had also received working capital from banks.

The unit collects its necessary raw materials mainly from local market and to some extent from Delhi.

It sells its products to the local market only. Usually, it produces tailor made goods.

There are 6 employees-4 full timer and 2 part timer. All the workers were recruited locally.

Working Results : Operating results indicate that year after year the performance of the unit deteriorated. It has been noted from the financial data that the unit reached break even point in 1973 i.e. after 3 years of starting commercial production. The performance of the unit increased till 1983, when the unit could utilise 60% of capacity. Thereafter the performance of the unit deteriorated significantly. In 1983, due to lack of order and working capital it could use only 10% of production capacity, which was 20% in 1985. Since 1986 this unit was running at loss and declared as a sick unit. However, it has been reported by the entrepreneur that he had received some good orders (1985-86) and quite hopeful of pulling up the unit from its sickness.

Constraints : The major problems confronted by the unit are lack of order for the goods, lack of raw materials, working capital and shortage of power supply. The unit manufacture tailor made goods and usually supply to the Government Departments. However, for the last few years it was not receiving sufficient order from them.

Working capital constraint is, severe one. In fact, at the time of interview the unit got a big order but was short of working capital and desperately searching for it.

The unit depends on local market for raw material, but the supply is irregular. It has also reported power problems and indifference of officials about its genuine problems.

CASE STUDY -9 : A Traders Unit

The Entrepreneur : The entrepreneur is a 55 year old trader. He is a non-matric and a retail trader in jute goods. None of his family members was having any manufacturing industry. His children are also in business but none of them are highly educated. The important motivating factor was to gain social status and respectability as an industry owner. The entrepreneur belongs to a non-backward district of Maharashtra state. He was not having any technical or educational experience in this line, though had got sufficient experience in marketing.

Location of the Unit : The unit was established in 1981 in a Government industrial area in a non-backward district of Maharashtra which is neither a developed, nor a backward but a developing district in Maharashtra selected for state Government subsidy only. It is not entitled for central Government incentives. But industrial land is available at cheaper rate.

The location decision of the entrepreneur was mainly influenced by the availability of industrial shed and his home town. Cheap labour was another consideration. However, it appeared that the primary factor was personal i.e., nearer to home town. He would have got more subsidy by locating his unit in a nearby backward district which is less than 200 kms from present location.

Capital, Employment etc. : The initial project cost of the unit was 2.5 lacs, out of which 10% was received as subsidy, 50% was received from commercial banks as loan and 40% was his own contribution.

The unit manufacture ropes and yarn for which 75% raw materials is collected from the region the rest being collected from outside the state (mainly from Calcutta). About 90% of the products sold outside the district and only 10% is sold in the district.

This unit has employed 33 persons out of which 13 are skilled labour and 20 unskilled. There were 22 local employees and 11 were outsiders.

Constraints : The unit has reported about the problem of raw materials and skilled labour. Raw material supply is very irregular and frequent shortage caused under utilisation of productive capacity. There was also the shortage of skilled workers. They demand wage at the rate of skilled labour in comparative industry in Poona. Moreover, working capital problem was occasionally experienced by the entrepreneur in spite of being an established trader in the area and having good contact with banks.

CASE STUDY - 10 : A Non-Resident Unit

The Entrepreneurs : The unit under discussion has been promoted by 3 non-resident technologists from the U.S.A. All three were in their early 40's. Out of 3, 2 are B.Tech. and were serving as engineer in U.S.A. for 8 years and third one, a Ph.D in Engineering was teaching in a U.S. university. Their families fully depended on income from service. It seems from the family background that they belong to upper middle class families.

These 3 technologists were well placed and well settled in the U.S.A. prior to starting this unit in India. Due to the desire to have more professional satisfaction, they were motivated to start their own industrial venture by giving up the well paid job in the U.S.A. The practical experience in the same line, and the growing Indian market also encouraged them to start this present project.

Location of the Unit : This private limited unit is registered under Factory Act. This unit has been located in a non-backward district of U.P. The only location factor they considered was the location of their home town. The unit was established in 1977 and commercial production started in 1978. They manufacture custom made sophisticated machinery which are usually imported in India.

Capital, Employment etc. : The total project of (land building machinery) the unit was Rs. 17.48 lacs out of which about 18% was contributed by promoters about 58% was received from the U.P.F.C. and the rest from commercial banks. Except term loan and working capital, the unit did not receive any other assistance from Government agencies.

We have observed a strong backward linkage in respect of employment. The unit has 110 persons including managers, office staffs, skilled and unskilled workers. Out of 110, only 35 were unskilled. Out of 110, 75 employees belong to the town and 35 were outsiders.

But the material linkage is directed outside the regions, because the unit collects 70% of raw material from other states and 10% are imported from abroad.

Operating Results : According to the promoters, the operating results are quite satisfactory and the unit is making profit for the last few years. The unit reached break even point in 1979 and it is utilising full installed capacity. We have also noted a progressive trend of growth of sales as well as net profit.

Constraints : The promoters have not reported any major problems, except shortage of water and insufficient power supply. It seems from the discussions with the promoters that they are quite satisfied with services of the various government agencies.

Some Observations About Case Studies

The cases examined above indicate the emerging trend of entrepreneurship development in small and medium scale sector. However, it should be admitted that the No. of cases examined is too small and no claim can be made to have presented entire picture. Yet these cases have indicated that the emerging entrepreneurial class consist of people from various socio-economic strata, motivated by different achievement objects and in the process experienced different problems. We can sum up the important points that have emerged out of the examination of above cases:

1. The new entrepreneurs have come from different socio-economic strata. Their age, qualification and experience also differ from each other. However, we have noted that the entrepreneurs having link to trade/industry usually preferred to locate their units in non-backward urban centres. These traders businessmen turned entrepreneures have better access to resources and are less dependent on institutional finance, whereas, technocrats/professional entrepreneurs have less access to financial resources and preferred to go to backward regions in order to avail Government incentives and concessional finance.

2. In general, a high degree of achievement, motivation has been noted among the entrepreneurs but the innovative and non-monetary achievement factors induced the majority of entrepreneurs in backward regions. Further, the entrepreneurs are primarily self motivated rather than motivated by institutionalised training/development programmes. However, institutional assistance acted as strong inducements, particularly to the entrepreneurs in backward regions.

3. Financial Institutions played a very crucial role to induce the potential entrepreneurs by supplying necessary financial capital. The availability of concessional finance and various incentives significantly influenced the location decision of the units particularly in backward regions. In the process, many of the entrepreneurs had overlook the other pre-requisites and factors for industrial location. Many of them were also unrealistically thought of the unlimited Government assistance. So, when that was not available they could not stand on their own to fight the challenges of several constraints.

4. The industrial units are usually small in size (in terms of investment as well as employment) particularly in backward regions. Most of the industries promoted by the first generation entrepreneurs are 'Foot-loose' type high-capital intensive and have strong forward linkage.

There is absence of local resource based and labour intensive units. Therefore, export based regional development is not taking place in backward and rural regions. It has also been noted from the questionnaire that inter industry linkage is very weak, as most of the industrial units in our sample are independent of other large units in the region.

5. Product selection and marketability are important factors exerting considerable influence on growth, and profitability of any industry. But in our sample we observe that the selection of the product was not always judicious.

We have also noted that many units could not create alternative market for their products. Therefore, when the assured market was lost they sank and gradually became sick. The new industries, particularly the small scale units do not receive any substantial and effective marketing assistance from government agencies. Therefore, they can not expand the market beyond the locality and region.

6. Labour and raw materials are the other areas of concern for these new units. There is general problem of shortage of skilled labour in backward areas. Labour turnover is a big problem particularly for small industries in Maharashtra (sample sector).

7. We have already noted that there is absence of local raw material based industries. As a result, a very high percentage of units depended on, outside district/state for raw materials which not only increased the cost of procurement, but also hampered smooth operation of units due to irregularity in supply. Supply from state agency is not very satisfactory.

8. We have also noted from our interview with the entrepreneurs that the infrastructure posed a major problems to the growth. Particularly in backward regions. Lack of communication and transportation facilities, irregular power and water supply, absence of residential accommodations, education, health, recreation facilities etc., are the major infrastructural problems. Poor infrastructure increased the production cost. Due to poor social infrastructure industries are also not able to attract qualified people. However, in non-backward regions, the infrastructure is comparatively well developed.

9. Finally the most of the units examined above complaint about the lack of healthy co-operation and proper assistance from Government agencies involved in implementing various schemes of Government incentives.

6

TOWARDS AN ENTREPRENEURIAL DEVELOPING SOCIETY

Introduction

Evaluation and assessment of Entrepreneurial Development Programme (EDP) in the light of field data and published reports indicate that not much headway could be made to establish an entrepreneurial developing society in India. There are several factors responsible for it. However, the most important being : absence of proper direction, priority and lack of coordination among multifarious agencies involved in EDP, absence of infrastructure and national thrust; absence of spontaneous participation and involvement of people; absence of industrial culture and entrepreneurial environment; absence of stable and interconnected economic industrial and educational policy in the country.

Entrepreneurship is a natural process—develop out of demographic characteristics, economic constraints and opportunities, educational and technical changes etc. Favourable development of these factors influence the outlook of individual and society and bring attitudinal change conducive to the entrepreneurial growth. But, in India hardly any effort has been made towards this aspect of entrepreneurial development under any long-term policy perspective. Economic, educational and technical changes which exert more influence on individual and social outlook are very slow and loosely connected. Therefore, they failed to generate any dynamism in Indian Society.

Ignoring the long-term perspective of developing entrepreneurial society we have increasingly relied on adhok efforts and popularist measures to achieve short-term objectives to promote so-called entrepreneurs through incentives, assistance and training programmes. Even the short-term measures which have been initiated for immediate gains could not deliver any significant result due to inbuilt weakness, short-sightedness of the programmes and trainers. EDP has failed, because programmes are not designed scientifically under Indian socio-cultural and economic condition. Elitist trainers and experts under the influence of Western educational experience have tried to mould the rural people brought up in a different value system and cultural environment. There always remained a wide gap between trainer and trainee. Naturally, nothing could be absorbed effectively.

Another impeding factor is Babu culture in India. Babu culture, which was cleverly developed by colonial rulers in India to prevent growth of nationalism, development of economy and self-reliance is by nature anti-innovative, anti-dynamic and anti-achievement oriented. This culture, prevented growth of entrepreneurial environment and industrial culture, limited the scope of self-advancement of achievement oriented people. We must have to do away with this babus and babu culture.

The semi urban attitudes of the Babus, and the so-called western outlook ignored the realities of wide socio-economic disparities between urban and rural areas. Therefore, while framing programmes for entrepreneurial development they ignored localised factors and the EDP remained alien to our rural and backward areas. There is lack of involvement and spontaneous participation of local people. The programme failed to enlarge its scope to identify potential entrepreneurs from different strata of society to induce achievement, motivation and mobility and to develop need based result oriented schemes of training and incentives. The ultimate result is insufficient response, slow growth, and early death of entrepreneurship.

Summarised findings of field study can be used to analyse the slow entrepreneurial growth (in terms of emerging entrepreneurial type, motivation and mobility and efficacy of EDP, incentives etc.) We have further discussed about the factors responsible for early death of entrepreneurship and finally presented a frame work of structural planning for developing an entrepreneurial society in India by keeping all the socio-economic factors into account.

Emerging Entrepreneurial Class

(a) **Type of Entrepreneur**

Out of 122 entrepreneurs examined, 72 i.e. 59% of entrepreneurs are below 40 yrs. Out of 72, 50 i.e. 69% are located in backward areas and 22 i.e. 31% are located in non-backward areas. Statewise analysis indicate that in U.P., out of 80 entrepreneurs, 48 (i.e. 60%) are upto 40 yrs, while in Maharashtra, 24 out of 42 (i.e. 57%) are in the same age group. Therefore, first generation entrepreneurs in U.P. are comparatively in the lower age group.

The first generation entrepreneurs in our sample are better educated. About 60% are Graduates and 24% are Post Graduate which indicate a high level of formal educational background. Moreover, about 30% of the above are technically qualified. The percentage of technically qualified entrepreneurs was higher in Maharashtra than in U.P.

The sample data also give an indication of past experience of the entrepreneurs. 73% had the past experience. 33% have worked in the same line and 40% in the other lines, and 27% had no experience.

Age, education and experience of entrepreneurs indicate that a younger band of qualified, particularly technically qualified entrepreneurs with reasonable past experience are emerging in India where the entrepreneurship was the domain of low-educated family bound traditional profession. Therefore, emerging trend is very much encouraging for a developing country like India.

(b) Motivation and Mobility

(i) Motivation : This study has indicated that achievement motivation is quite high among Indian entrepreneurs. This argument is based on the facts that in spite of poor financial background and lack of access to resources, many young people left their well secured job to venture into entrepreneurial world-full of risk and uncertainty. Out of 122 entrepreneurs, 32 (i.e. 26%) were motivated by monetary factors, while 54 (i.e. 44%) were motivated by the non-monetary factors like social recognition, independence, responsibility and self advancement. While 21, (i.e. 17%) took up entrepreneurship as a means of employment. The former factors are the qualities of creative entrepreneurs, the later category of entrepreneurs can be called 'forced entrepreneurship'. This category of people taken up entrepreneurship due to unemployment problem. However, considering the percentage of entrepreneurs of first 2 categories (0.5%), we can say that the emerging entrepreneurial class is highly creative and has high degree of achievement motivation.

(ii) Mobility : Entrepreneurship offers the best opportunity for self-advancement and social mobility. Successful entrepreneurial development programme is expected to attract entrepreneurs from various social and economic strata of society. India has achieved considerable success in this respect. In our sample, entrepreneurs with non-trading business background was more than 50%. We have noted that 48.4% entrepreneurs were from families of traders, business men, 9% from agriculturist families, 42.6% from families which depend on service and other profession activities.

It is, therefore, significant that a very high per cent of entrepreneurs have participated from non-business background. However, most discouraging feature is the failure of the present programme to attract a sizeable No. of entrepreneurs from agriculturists in rural areas. This indicates that agricultural income, instead of channelising into manufacturing is utilised for some other purposes.

The traditional hold of business/trading families over the manufacturing activities is gradually breaking down and a new generation of highly qualified creative entrepreneurial class is emerging from cross section of people.

This new generation entrepreneurs are achievement oriented and do not mind to move outside their home region if opportunities are available. In our sample, 52 out of 122 (i.e. 42.6%) entrepreneurs had migrated from other places. This high percentage of outsiders is also a support to our hypothesis that the first generation entrepreneurs in India is highly achievement oriented.

(c) Impact of Training and Incentives

(i) Training : We have seen that a No. of agencies have been engaged to identify, train and develop entrepreneurs, particularly in rural and backward areas. Every year, a good No. of highly qualified youngmen are coming forward to receive entrepreneurship training. But, what happened after training programme? How many actually established their enterprise after the EDP. No reliable information is available to quantify the impact of EDP. So we have made an attempt to see the impact of EDP with the help of scattered data that is available from various sources.

It has been stated in the Annual Report of IDBI (1984-85) that the TCOs, Banks, NSTEDP, EDII and other accredited agencies have trained over 12,200 entrepreneurs through EDP conducted by them. 'Out of these, only 25% to 30% entrepreneurs have already set up units while a few more at the Planning stage.'

Another information collected through one of the TCOs shows that out of 290 EDP conducted in 1984-85, in backward districts of a state, only 64 entrepreneurs (i.e. about 22% of the trained entrepreneurs) have established their units. Information collected from one of the regional centres of SISI shows that during 1984-85, and 1985-86, they have trained 213 and 178 entrepreneurs respectively. Out of these 391 trained entrepreneurs, only 296 have registered with DIC's i.e. only 76% have taken the first step to register with DIC's. Out of these 296, only 46 entrepreneurs have established their units and 115 units were in the process of establishment. Therefore, if all the units which were in process of establishment by the end of December 86 are established, only 40% of the entrepreneurs will be successful in establishing their enterprise.

It can, also be noted that about 20% to 30% of the entrepreneurs, who are trained through EDP, actually start their enterprise. This is not very encouraging picture. A very high percentage of trainees actually do not turn into entrepreneurs. This can be called as 'infant mortality of the entrepreneurship' which is quite high in India, particularly, in backward regions. It has been reported by one organization that they call the trainees after 2 to 3 months but only 'around 50% contact them. Again these trainees (entrepreneurs) are called after 3/4 months but not more than 25% to 30% respond. This agency provides post training counselling and guidance (free of charge). Even then, a large No. of trained people do not come forward for guidance and counselling.

(ii) Incentives : Incentives played a very crucial role in inducing the first generation entrepreneurs (particularly from non-business class) to start their own industrial units. One of the major problems in India is the lack of financial capital required for establishing industries. However, due to the availability of subsidies and concessional finance many first generation entrepreneurs could enter into manufacturing as entrepreneurs. In absence of financial capital these entrepreneurs would have remained dormant. Moreover, non-financial incentives like cheaper land, constructed sheds, concessional power, water, etc. also acted as 'pull factors' for the first generation entrepreneurs. The incentives however, was more

inducing for the entrepreneurs in backward regions than for their counter parts in non-backward regions.

It has been revealed in our study that 35% units were basically influenced by financial incentives and 25% by non-financial incentives. It is, therefore, satisfying to note that 60% units in our sample were basically induced and established due to the availability of subsidies and other incentives.

Financial incentives have exerted stronger 'locational pull' in Maharashtra than in Uttar Pradesh. It is revealed in our study that 21 units (out of 35) in Maharashtra were primarily influenced by financial incentives including, subsidy and 7 units by non-financial incentives i.e. 60% and 20% units (total being 80%) in Maharashtra were induced to set up in the respective location. Above 21 units were heavily depended on Government and institutional assistance and could start their units due to availability of subsidies and incentives.

In U.P. 14 units out of 65 were primarily influenced by financial incentives and 18 were influenced by non-financial incentives. Therefore, 21.5% and 27.7% (total being 49.2%) units were induced by incentives. Incentives, therefore, exerted relatively less influence in U.P. The reasons for the comparatively lower degree of influence of incentives on location and entrepreneurial decision in U.P. was due to:

(a) A higher percentage of first generation entrepreneurs in U.P. came from business families having considerable financial backing.
(b) The group of entrepreneurs in U.P. are more tradition bound and desired less intervention from Government agencies. They, therefore, resorted to non-institutional assistance.
(c) Incentive administration is less efficient in U.P.
(d) Poor quality of development, and inefficient administration of infrastructure input in U.P. could not generate sufficient inducement among potential entrepreneurs.

Financial incentives though significantly motivated the first generation entrepreneurs, yet it suffered from the inbuilt weakness because no weightage was given to units promoted by the new entrepreneurs.

Early Death of Enterpreneurship

The experience of EDP has revealed, a discouraging trend of

very slow entrepreneurial growth and untimely death of entrepreneurship. Death of entrepreneurship takes place at several stages due to a variety of factors. These stages can broadly be divided into three categories namely—Initiation stage, Formation stage and Growth stage. Initiation stage can be defined as the period from conception to EDP training, Formation stage can be defined as the period from post training to establishment of a particular unit and the 'period from second to third year' can be treated as Growth stage. This approximation of period based on the experience as revealed by the first generation entrepreneurs during our field study. While the death of entrepreneurship during Initiation stage can be called as very early death, death during Formation and Growth stage can respectively be called as early death. We would like to discuss in brief the major factors responsible for early death and slow growth of entrepreneurship.

(a) Very Early Death

Most of the factors responsible for early death of entrepreneurship are entrepreneur related though the institutional factors have significant influence. We have identified the following major factors at this stage:

(i) *Lack of Goal:* Many trainees attend the programme (EDP) without any specific goal to establish industry in the post training period. They want to keep themselves busy during the transitory period between the end of academic life and beginning of employment. Therefore, entrepreneurial desire die with completion, even sometimes during training period.

(ii) *EDP as Status Symbol* : It was noted that many people who are usually less qualified think that by attending such training they would acquire academic status among friends and relatives. Therefore, their purposes are other than entrepreneurship and no entrepreneurial activities are initiated by them.

(iii) *Enhanced Employment Opportunity:* A section of trainees attend the training programme with an idea that the training would be treated as an additional qualification in the job market. Therefore, their intention is not to use the EDP training to start any industrial unit but to enhance their prospects in the job market.

The Role of Entrepreneurs in Backward Areas

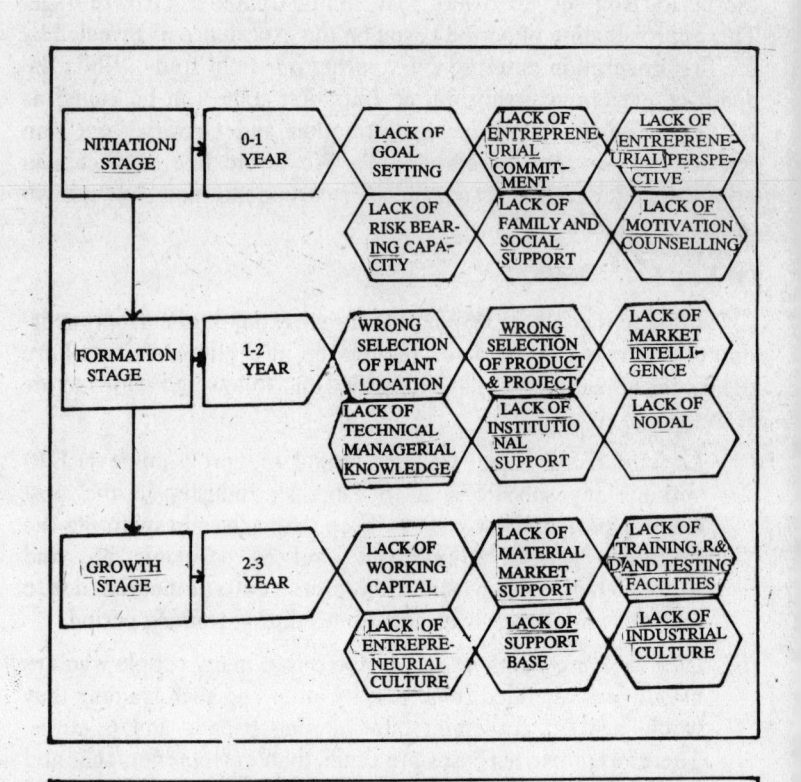

Stage	Duration	Factors
INITIATION STAGE	0-1 YEAR	LACK OF GOAL SETTING; LACK OF ENTREPRENEURIAL COMMITMENT; LACK OF ENTREPRENEURIAL PERSPECTIVE; LACK OF RISK BEARING CAPACITY; LACK OF FAMILY AND SOCIAL SUPPORT; LACK OF MOTIVATION COUNSELLING
FORMATION STAGE	1-2 YEAR	WRONG SELECTION OF PLANT LOCATION; WRONG SELECTION OF PRODUCT & PROJECT; LACK OF MARKET INTELLIGENCE; LACK OF TECHNICAL MANAGERIAL KNOWLEDGE; LACK OF INSTITUTIONAL SUPPORT; LACK OF NODAL
GROWTH STAGE	2-3 YEAR	LACK OF WORKING CAPITAL; LACK OF MATERIAL MARKET SUPPORT; LACK OF TRAINING, R&D AND TESTING FACILITIES; LACK OF ENTREPRENEURIAL CULTURE; LACK OF SUPPORT BASE; LACK OF INDUSTRIAL CULTURE

FACTORS INFLUENCING EARLY DEATH OF ENTREPRENEURSHIP

FIG-2

(iv) Entrepreneurs by Windfall: There are entrepreneurs in our sample who had no intention to take entrepreneurship but the problem of unemployment forced them to start industrial units. This type of entrepreneurs work only to survive and the society is not much benefitted through their lifeless endeavours.

(v) Lack of Motivation/Determination: Some trainees are easily influenced by the glamour of industrialists and propose to start their units after receiving training. They have the illusion to receive everything easily in the Post Training period. But reality is different and they cannot put the necessary hard work to see the project through due to lack of determination and achievement motivation.

(vi) Lack of Access to Resources: Sometimes achievement oriented and potential entrepreneurs after receiving EDP training are not able to establish their own project mainly due to lack of access to resources (particularly, financial resources). There are so many obstacles even in respect of Government assistance. Lack of contact causes severe delay at every steps. Institutiona-lization of corruption and unethical practices have creates hurdles for new entrepreneurs. Very often the potential entrepreneurs are bound to give up the idea of establishing own units.

(vii) Post Training Follow up: No serious efforts are made by the institutions/agencies to motivate the potential entrepreneurs after the training is over. Some formal efforts are made to contact the trainees, but no effective steps are taken to see what happened to trainees after completion of training. No proper track records are maintained, neither by the Government Department nor by the training institutions.

(viii) Lack of Support to Bear Risk : An Entrepreneur has to bear tremendous risk involving physical hardship and emotional strain. Entrepreneurial risk not only involve the entrepreneurs alone but his entire family. These risks can broadly be classified as :

(a) Career risks
(b) Financial risks
(c) Technical (Know-how) risks.

Venturing into entrepreneurship involve the career of a

person. Sometimes, he gives up lucrative and secured jobs for unforeseen future which may ruin his life. The entrepreneur put his hard earned money at stake (may be his life long savings) even at the sacrifice of the pleasure and comfort of family members. Technical/knowhow risk involved in entering into business or industry without much knowledge and skill of mechanical, financial and marketing aspects of the industry.

(b) **Early Death of Entrepreneurship**

There are several factors contributing entrepreneurial death during formation and growth stage. Some factors are entrepreneurial/organisation related while the other are related to various Government agencies. These factors can broadly be divided into two categories namely—internal and external. Let us see the major internal and external factors causing early death of entrepreneurship.

Internal Factors : Internal Factors which can be controlled by the management of the unit.

(a) Entrepreneur oriented factors
   (i) Low risk bearing capacity
   (ii) Low motivation
   (iii) Lack of technical knowledge
   (iv) Lack of training

(b) Production related factors
   (i) Location disadvantages
   (ii) High Cost of inputs
   (iii) Poor capacity utilisation
   (iv) Poor quality controls
   (v) Inadequate inventory
   (vi) Poor labour productivity
   (vii) High labour turnover
   (viii) Shortage of skilled labours
   (ix) Shortage of raw materials

(c) Market related factors
   (i) Inability to expand customers net work
   (ii) Weak market organisation and market feed back
   (iii) Inadequate marketing assistance

(d) Finance related factors
   (i) Lack of access to non-institutional finance
   (ii) Excessive dependence on financial institutions
   (iii) Inadequate working capital
   (iv) Non-availability of credit at right time
   (v) Delay in payment of customers
   (vi) Delay in loan sanction

External Factors: From the field data, the following external factors can be listed.

(a) Infrastructure oriented factors—shortage of power, water, transport and other critical raw materials.

(b) Government agency related factors
   (i) Delay in sanctioning loans, subsidies etc.
   (ii) Rigid institutional formalities.
   (iii) Absence of necessary cooperation from Government agencies.
   (iv) Lack of understanding of the problems of entrepreneur.

The entrepreneur related factors like risk bearing capacity, motivation and training are usually correlated factors. The degree of risk bearing and motivation depend on the social and economic background as well as development of support system. Entrepreneurs with trade/business background have better risk bearing capacity due to better external support.

Production related constraints are generally accelerated by the wrong selection of location, wrong projects, poor implementation and management. We have noted that several foot loose units have been established in backward areas mainly due to availability of subsidy and incentives and they suffered due to locational disadvantages. At that distant locations, the cost of production increased due to higher transport cost. Production suffered due to non-availability critical raw materials and other inputs.

Labour is yet another major problem. Productivity of labour is generally low in backward areas. Though labour unrest has generally been felt in non-backward areas, the labour turnover is a serious problem in backward areas, particularly at places where industries are developing very fast. Skilled labours are switching over to medium and large industries for better wages. Due to poor financial position the small scale units are generally facing the shortage even in non-backward areas. Problem of inadequate inventory was also observed in respect of small scale units in backward areas. Small units cannot maintain high inventory due to shortage of funds. Another problem which hampered growth, is the irregular supply of raw materials by the state agencies. In many cases, raw material shortage caused to be the primary factor for under-utilisation of installed capacity.

Marketing is a crucial problem for the small scale entrepreneurs. Marketing problems are many-fold. Lack of market intelligence, marketing knowledge, weak marketing net-work and absence of any worth-while marketing assistance from the Government agencies. Many small units manufacture high quality goods but due to lack of proper marketing channel, goods are not reaching to consumers.

Finance related constraints are lack of access to non-institutional finance, shortage of working capital delayed payment by large industries/distributors. The first generation entrepreneurs, who are from non-trading/families primarily suffer from shortage of credit. Many entrepreneurs—during field survey—bitterly complaint about the lack of cooperation, understanding and harassment from Banks. A sizeable No. of units have stated that shortage of working capital was the primary cause of under-utilisation of capacity and the cause of potential sickness.

The entrepreneurs have bitterly complaint about the problems caused by the external factors like lack of infrastructural facilities, Government apathy, harassment, and indifferency of Government officials.

Infrastructure is a really a major cause of concern in backward areas. We have noted that necessary and sufficient social and industrial infrastructural facilities do not exist in backward areas. Irregular power and water supply, poor communication, transportation, social facilities like school, college, hospital, recreation facilities and residential accommodations are not available in backward areas. While absence of industrial infrastructures increase the production cost, absence of social infrastructure act as disincentives for skilled labours and managerial personnels to go to backward areas.

While entrepreneurs have bitterly complained about commercial Banks, they are more or less happy with term lending institutions. But they speak about the indifference and unhelpful attitude of various administrative departments. Moreover, entrepreneurs in one industrial complex complaint about the non-fulfilment of Government promise to buy their products. More than 60% of the units in this complex are sick because they cannot sell their products in open market.

Some of the units have also complained about the long delay in disbursing Government subsidy. However, the complaint about Government agencies are more frequent in U.P. than in Maharashtra, where the entrepreneurs are more contended.

We have made an attempt to quantify the major constraints of growth of sample units. Out of 100 units, 61 are located in backward districts and 39 are located in non-backward districts. The common major problems are shortage of working capital, shortage of raw materials, marketing of products in both backward and non-backward districts. While 25.6% units in non-backward districts reported technical problem, only 19.7% units in backward districts reported this problem. Many such units have been promoted by non-technical persons, while most of the units in backward districts are recently established and promoter (entrepreneurs) are mostly young technocrats/professional with past experience in similar line. The problem of power and water supply are also more in non-backward districts. The shortage of skilled labour and problem of transportation have been reported by more units in backward districts because such locations are far away from city centres.

Further break up of the sample units between U.P. and Maharashtra indicate that the intensity of the problems is more in U.P. than in Maharashtra in case of most of the factors considered by us. While 56.9% of units in U.P. have the problem of shortage of working capital, only 22.6% units in Maharashtra have reported this problem. Shortage of raw materials and marketing problems are also more in U.P. than in Maharashtra. More units in U.P. have also suffered due to shortage of power and water supply. This is because the infrastructure is better developed in Maharashtra than in U.P. in general and backward areas in particulars. Transport problems are more or less similar in U.P. and Maharashtra. However, shortage of skilled labour is more in Maharashtra, is due to high turnover. Labour troubles are also more in small units in Maharashtra because the rate of wage in similar industries in developed centres as well as for similar jobs in large units are very high and secondly due to more organised labour movement in Maharashtra. Apart from individual cases of sick units, we have noted that even a well-intended industrial complex is tending towards sickness.

In one industrial complex (located in a backward district) 12 industrial units were set up few years back. At the time of our interview in 1986, 4 units were closed, 4 units were declared as 'sick' and remaining 4 were merely surviving. The reasons, as stated by the entrepreneurs, were non-fulfilment of promise by the State Government to buy their products, poor infrastructure and lack of marketing facilities. This type of sickness not only discourages the new entrepreneurs but also create unproductive burden on exchequer. This problem should have been attended with sincerity and care but no efforts have been made by any agency to solve the problems of this 'complex'.

The First Generation Entrepreneurs, as noted from the above, are confronted with several institutional and non-institutional constraints which have impeded entrepreneurial augmentation and industrial growth.

With the bad experience of those, who have already started their units and are facing lot of difficulties, the potential young entrepreneurs are getting discouraged. Therefore, the demotivating factors are to be removed in order to promote quality entrepreneurship in the country. Since the problems are manifold and multidimensional, we have to initiate concrete efforts to remove those detriments to growth and development of new entrepreneurs. The agenda of action should be directed with a total view of the problems. The piecemeal actions would not be able to solve the problems of new entrepreneurs.

A Structural Planning Model

It has been noted that entrepreneurial development and augmentation are impeded by several endogenous and exogenous factors (as well as the shortsightedness of the present model of EDP being practiced in India). The problem is so enormous and our policies are so narrow, no tangible result could be achieved by making some changes here and there. If we seriously desire to bring some changes, we have to develop a perspective and bring a conceptual change through rationalisation and restructurisation of development model. We have to adopt an integrated approach under broader perspective of social change which must facilitate to develop industrial culture and entrepreneurial environment.

In order to overcome the structural problems, we have to initiate multi-dimensional policy measures to remove the hindrances to entrepreneurial growth under a rationalised and structured policy frame work. The measures should be able to remove the shortcomings of existing policies and programmes as well as aim at evolving a dynamic socio-economic system which would facilitate to develop industrial culture and entrepreneurial environment for natural growth of entrepreneurship. The desired model should aim at:

(a) Structural change of backward areas through utilisation of local resources.
(b) Developing institutional infrastructure and institutions to identify, train and motivate entrepreneurs.
(c) Developing suitable strategy to identify train and motivate potential entrepreneurs.
(d) Evolving more suitable incentives for entrepreneurs.
(e) Creating better access to capital and critical raw materials and infrastructure (social and industrial).
(f) Inducing innovation and technological adaptability.
(g) Inducing private initiative through reward creation of congenial environment conducive to self-advancement and growth.
(h) Improvement of image of self-employment, status of business and businessman.
(i) Removal of colonial hang-ups on salaried employment and concept of superiority of administrative jobs.
(j) Re-designing education plan to enhance the importance and utility of vocational education.
(k) Creating industrial culture and entrepreneurial environment.

The objectives that are mentioned above cannot be achieved overnight or in a short-cut method. To attain these, we need a well designed policy frame-work and suitable instruments which are applicable to Indian condition. Our economic measures must create employment opportunities for unemployed and disguised unemployed and ensure equity in distribution of wealth and income. Our industrial policy must create an environment for private initiative as well fuller utilisation of Indian resources and ensure distribution of gains through industrialisation. Our educational policy should develop initiative, innovativeness, dignity and spirit of entrepreneurship. It should produce highly achievement oriented people. Human Resource Development Policy, which is closely linked to Education

Policy must be designed to exploit country's manpower potential and create an environment for self advancement. Appropriate training at all levels must be initiated to develop and improve the hidden potential of manpower. Such a policy perspective is necessary to increase supply of creative innovative and achievement oriented entrepreneurs who are not merely profit seekers but act as agent of socio-economic change in a society.

Further, the element of involvement is the most important characteristics of any programme designed to bring lasting change in any segment of society. In our programme of entrepreneurship in backward areas this link between the programme and people is missing. The Western Oriented programme has very little link to local people and as such there is very little scope of participation. Even, type of industries being setup in rural and backward areas could offer little to local society. Therefore, our training and development programme must be able to attract local people and their spontaneous participation, involvement in development as well as EDP activities. The rural people has to accept our programme mentally and to work for its success. Any attempt to make shift change will be fruitless. An environment has to be created to make the people aware of the necessity of change, otherwise it is difficult to convince them to what entrepreneurship means.

The scheme therefore, emphasised upon the necessity of inducing industrial culture, industrial training and education and developing growth mentality among the people of rural areas. This growth mentality and industrial culture can be developed in the rural areas if the people see some gain in it. We, emphasise upon the increasing in purchasing power through employment of rural resource and manpower. Rural resources including manpower can be fully exploited if resource based and employment intensive industries are established. If some industries in rural areas are established which depend on outside supply of raw materials and manpower, the effect of income employment multiplier is directed outside the region. If so happen, the local people may not be interested in such development. Since the involvement is the cornerstone of success of any development programme, local people may be made to involve in any programme which are taken for bringing a change in the socio-economic structure of the region. The scheme has therefore, emphasised upon creating conditions for self-actualisation of the local potential entrepreneurs. Through developing Territorial Industries.

FIG - 3

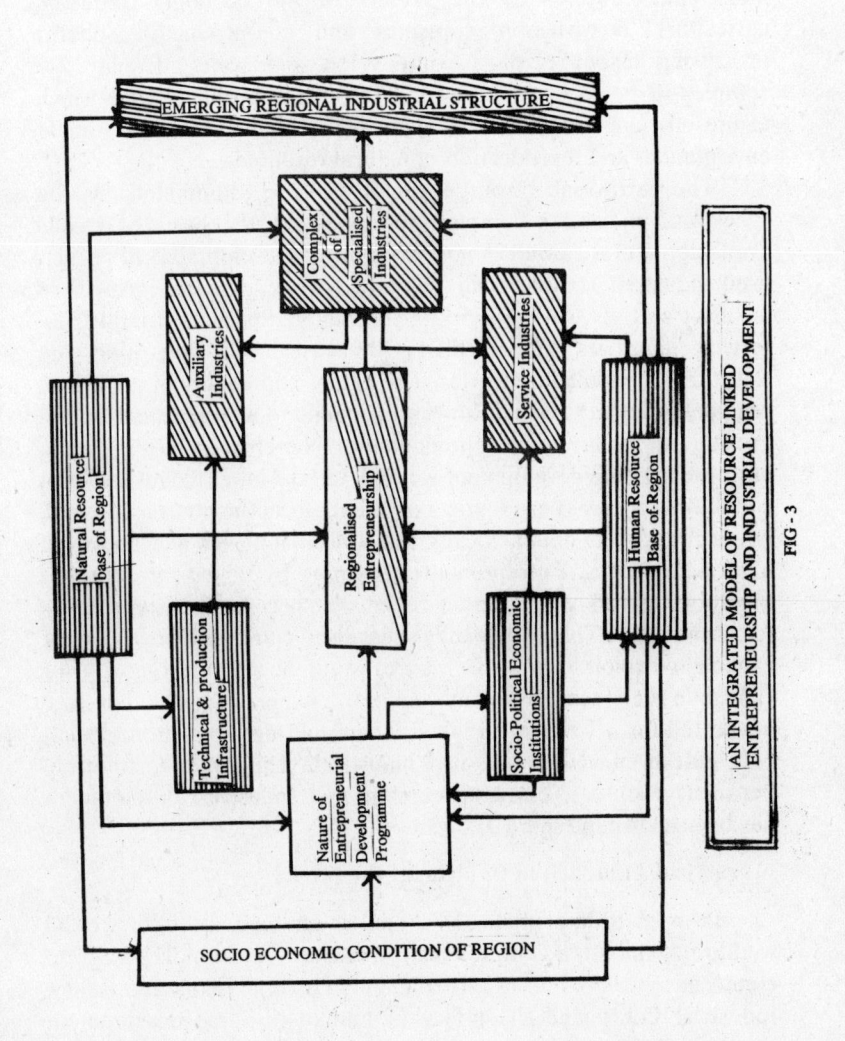

AN INTEGRATED MODEL OF RESOURCE LINKED ENTREPRENEURSHIP AND INDUSTRIAL DEVELOPMENT

One of the most important aspect of the scheme is the identification of 'Territorial Resource Region' and establishment of 'Rural Industrial Institutes' with a view to develop resource based territorial industrial complex. According to M.K. Badman a territorial industrial complex is a planned proportionately developing aggregate of stably interconnected units of the sectors of the economy (industry, agriculture, construction, transport and non-productive sphere) processing resources of a composition and scale adequate for complex to be involved in solving the major problems and which insure efficient use of local and outside resources conservation of environment and reproduction of natural resources.

The territorial resource region will be dominated by the specialised industries complex developed on the basis of locally available natural resources and manpower. Development of specialised industrial complex will assist and necessitate the growth of auxiliary and service industries in the region. Specialised industries, service industries and auxiliary industries will determine the structure of regional industries. The extent and quality of growth of regional industries, would, however, depend to a large extent on the growth and quality of entrepreneurship. Therefore, while initiating entrepreneurship development we have to take into account the local condition i.e., socio-economic condition, local institutions (social, political and economic), locally available manpower and above all natural resources. Entrepreneurial training by taking into account the above factors will promote regionally specialised entrepreneurs for each region. These regionally specialised entrepreneurs are more capable to exploit local resources and would be able to bring a faster change in socio-economic condition of the region. We have therefore advocated for a Resource Linked integrated model to promote not only entrepreneurship but also industries. This inter-relationship between resources, entrepreneurship and industrial development has been shown in Figure 3.

A Practical Approach to Implement the Model

In order to implement the model as outlined above, first of all we have to initiate a comprehensive measures at the policy stage to create an entrepreneurial environment. General Economic Policy, Industrial Policy and the policy of human resource development should be formed in such a way as to develop enterprising creative, innovativeness right from the days of childhood. Incentives for

FIG - 4

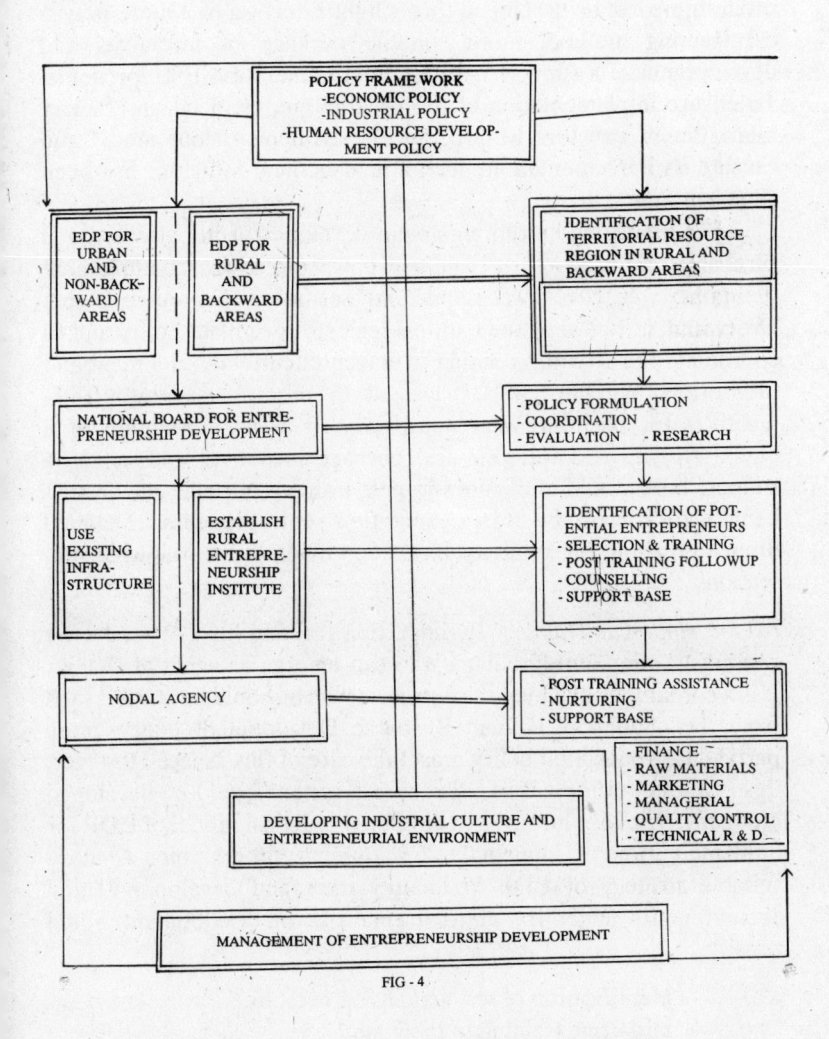

private and initiatives innovation and a special thrust on development of backward areas to be developed through utilisation of regional resources. Further, the policy measures should be able to establish correlation between entrepreneurial development and training, regional resources and production system. However such a programme can be developed through introduction of a more practical training method, more suitable package of incentives and development of a support base for First Generation Entrepreneurs. To ensure implementation of the programme, we need an efficient management structure to integrate the elements of our model and execute its implementation. Such a management structure has been shown in Figure 4.

For managing entrepreneurship development in backward and rural areas we need a thrust and new policy directives. To implement the policy objectives we require to set up a Entrepreneurship Development Board at the national level, to formulate policy and to coordinate the activities relating to entrepreneurial development and promotion. We have also suggested to promote separate EDP, institutes for backward and non-backward areas. Formation of a Nodal Agency to deal with new package incentives and act as a support base would eliminate the post-training obstacles at present being confronted by first generation entrepreneurs. Detailed discussion about these factors have been made in the following subsections:

(a) Development Training: By imparting training for 2/3 weeks, we can not develop entrepreneurs who can emerge as agent of change. It is a continuous and long-term process which should be started right from the childhood. Human Resource Development policy, more particularly education policy must take care of this aspect. However, this is a long-term measures and such a system would be developed gradually. We have however to develop a practical model of EDP for implementation of immediate development programme. A more suitable strategy of EDP to identify train and develop potential entrepreneurs under the above framework of development would consist:

— identification of self-actualising persons,
— imparting training to them, and
— advancing post training assistance.

Identification of self-actualising persons to make them successful entrepreneurs through entrepreneurship training and post training assistance should be done very carefully. Only the self-actualising persons with high degree of survival instinct and achievement motivation are to be selected through a scientifically designed psychological test. The test should be designed to assess the self-actualisation and survival instinct, i.e.

— The potential skill and capacity,
— Desire to utilise his skill and capacity in a mature way,
— Potential to fight the odds,
— Traditionally acquired skill, and
— Attitude toward socially oriented commercial and development activities.

While preference may be given to those who have traditional art and craft background, business background and other having strong urge for mobility, the persons with only self interest may be eliminated. For the eligibility of selection, the person should atleast pass the High School Examination and should not be more than 25 years old. These persons will be trained in a specially designed Institute for Rural Entrepreneurs (IRE).

Institute for Rural Entrepreneurship

This specialised institute will only cater to the needs of rural and backward areas. They will produce not only the entrepreneurs but the development workers and agents of social change and act as nodal centres for industrial growth and economic development.

Location of the Institute

These institutes will be located in rural areas at least 100 kms. away from city centres. For selecting location of the IREs, rural/backward areas will be divided into several 'Territorial Resource Regions' (TRR). One TRR may comprise 3/5 districts depending on the climate and resource conditions. These TRRs may be rich in mineral resources, forest resources, water resources, agricultural resources having the potentiality to develop the regions through development of industries on the basis of the local resources. This concept of territorial resource region is akin to the concept of developing export based industries.

Programme of Training

The IREs will impart 2 years integrated training to the selected potential entrepreneurs. Training will be free of the cost and all the training expenses including the cost of training materials will be born by the Government. Trainees will also be given Rs. 250/300 as out of pocket expenses.

The entrepreneurs will be trained with a view to create enough potentiality among the trainees to start local resource based and demand based industries. Three types of industries can be promoted in each region on the basis of local resources.

— Specialised Industry (the main industry using the primary local resource as raw materials).
— Auxiliary Industries (those industries need to provide the operating conditions of the specialised industries).
— Service Industries (Industries providing necessary services to specialised and auxiliary industries).

To start with 20/25 trainees may be selected and trained, in each of the above industries for making them prepared to start industries in one of the above categories. After successful completion of training, the candidates will be given certificates which will be the passport for them to enter into industrial field. This certificate will be used for:

— Acquiring land/sheds etc.
— For term loan/working capital loan etc. from financial institutes and banks.
— For acquiring raw material on preferential basis.

Course Contents

The course of the training at IRE will be entirely different from traditional training. The course will be designed in such a way that it would:

(i) induce and enhance self-actualisation,
(ii) achievement motivation,
(iii) social needs,
(iv) use of resources,
(v) create technology mentality,
(vi) prepare development workers.

The course contents may be divided into 3 categories:

(i) Economic Aspects:
- General Economy
- Regional Economy
- Availability of regional raw material, manpower — climate — scope for various socialised auxiliary industries and service industries.

(ii) Technological Aspects:
- Basic Sciences
- Industrial Technology
- Requirement of technology to promote specialised and auxiliary and service industries
- Agricultural Technology
- Use of various primary machines
- Quality control etc.

(iii) Management Aspects:
- Finance management, production management, inventory management, labour management etc.

Study Tour

This will be a part of 2 years training programmes. The trainees will be taken to various plants in India and abroad not only to acquaint them with various management aspects but also to induce them to take up manufacturing and industrial entrepreneurship. Study tours will reinforce the self-actualisation of the trainees.

Study Tour in India will be in the form of inplant training for 3 to 6 months during the entire period of training. In plant training may be in 2 stages.

Stage I

This will be arranged after one year's basic training in technological, mechanical and other production aspects. If the trainees are deputed to plants (after they acquire basic knowledge in above aspects) they will gain practical knowledge and experience to handle operate and manage the machinery etc. as well as they will know what is what:

Stage II

Second study tour will be in the second year—once they acquire basic knowledge in management aspects. The trainees will be deputed to small and medium scale industries and be allowed to work during the tour along with managers and entrepreneurs. They will, at this stage, learn to work as a coordinator and manager. However, units should be selected very carefully. The successful entrepreneurs with good track records should selected for training.

Foreign Study Tour

This can be arranged immediately after second study tour in India. Foreign study tour may be for a week or so. The objective of this tour is to acquaint the trainees with the development and application of science and technology productivity and quality consciousness in industries particularly in small scale sector. This will induce the entrepreneurs to introduce new technology in Indian industries.

Developing Traineers

We have to discard the present practice of imparting training through elitist experts who are misfit in rural areas because of their basic attitude towards training which puts more emphasis on Theory than on practical utility of such training in rural areas. We do not require MBA or CA or Economists. What we require are committed people to train our young entrepreneurs. We may even select village craftsmen and train to make them trainers. We may invite simple business people and entrepreneurs as guest faculty at IREs. People who will be able to establish them with the potential entrepreneurs are the best traineers—and they should be promoted.

Post Training Follow-ups

At present a large number of young people are given so called 'entrepreneurship training' every year, particularly to fulfil the target of the training institutions and development agencies like TCOs, SISI etc. But, there is hardly any post training assistance and follow-up. We have already indicated in this study that merely 20-22% trainees actually set up their own units, which indicates huge waste of public money. We have to arrest this unhealthy situation through effective post training follow-up and assistance.

A system of follow-up counselling need to introduced. Follow-up counselling would help the trainee entrepreneur to:

(a) Select the product according to his capacity.
(b) Prepare Scientific Project Profile.
(c) Select appropriate location for the project.
(d) Select profile of the consumer and users of the product.
(e) Select appropriate marketing strategy for the products.
(f) Select source of Term Loan and Working Capital.

Counselling also provide information to the entrepreneurs about the following:

(a) Available range of complementary and substitute goods of his products.
(b) Market share of the existing firms.
(c) Likely change of National and International demand for the products due to R & D efforts in this field.
(d) Likely change in the Economic and Industrial policy of the Government.

Counselling should be broad based and intensive. Experts who are particularly trained in the field should be assigned for result oriented counselling.

IDBI has introduced a scheme titled as 'Follow Up Counselling' for EDP participants under which the TCOs in backward states would be entitled to claim subsidy for providing services to those who have successfully completed training conducted by TCOs and have got their loan sanctioned for setting up a unit in a notified backward area.

However, our experience shows that no sincere post training follow up and counselling is done. We have contacted three different institutions to check up the data about Post Training Follow up but no reliable data could be provided by them. This area of EDP, therefore, calls for more attention. Training institutions (here IRE) have to initiate close monitoring of post training follow up to see the problems of trainees to set up their units and to render necessary counselling. A suitable follow up machinery can be developed by calling the trainees every month for first 3 months. If necessary centrewise meeting of entrepreneurs who reside at distant places can be arranged. For this the concept of *BARE FOOT TRAINER* can be introduced. This trainer will meet the trainees at their residence in case they do not respond to the call of the institutions.

Post Training Assistance: Nodal Agency

Post-training follow ups and efficient counselling induce the trainees and motivate them to start their own units. But there are lot of hurdles to overcome. In fact hurdles are so many and so difficult to overcome, many trained people give up the idea of establishing their units. Registration, licencing, arrangement of land, finance, raw materials, machinery etc. are sometimes seems to be insurmountable. Even after the establishment of the unit and starting of production these problems exist. During our field study, most of the entrepreneurs have brought these problems to our notice, which are primarily—due to multiplicity of organisation and no business attitude of the dealing persons.

The first generation small entrepreneurs have to generally manage a one man show. The owner entrepreneur has to arrange capital, raw materials, marketing and all other odd jobs by himself. As a result a large part of available time is wasted. This problem can be solved through operation of a Nodal Agency. The budget of Government of India for 1988-89 indicated the formation of a Small Industries Development Bank and single window clearance of Term Loan and working capital for small industries. It is not yet clear what type of function this bank would perform. However, we would like to suggest that a Nodal Agency to coordinate the above activities for the entrepreneur is a must and many of the factors retarding entrepreneurial growth can be removed. The function/objective to form the Nodal Agency will be to assist entrepreneur through arranging land/industrial shed, finance, raw materials, plant & machinery, selling products, quality control and managerial assistance etc. The Nodal Agency should also take the lead in forming 'Industrial Cooperatives' through first generation entrepreneurs.

Though this Nodal Agency will function at the state it will be guided by the National Board for Entrepreneurial Development. For carrying out its function at the local level in the rural areas the Institute for Rural Entrepreneurial (IRE) can work as Nodal Centre. The Nodal Agency will also act as a support base for entrepreneurs and will attempt to rationalise various Government schemes of incentives and assistance. We discuss below some of the important areas requiring close attention of the proposed Nodal Agency:

Finance and Incentives

Finance is the critical input for new and small units, and the Financial agencies have initiated verious scheme to assist such units. There are various suitable schemes for term loan and working capital for first generation entrepreneurs. However, though operation of financial institutes are quite satisfactory, the first generation entrepreneurs are not very satisfied with commercial banks and the problem of working capital is very acute. Shortage of working capital and delay in sanction have affected several new units. In order to remove these problems we suggest to establish a small scale financial corporation, which would look after the short term and long term and new units. This corporation will also administer the incentive schemes of central and state government. This organisation will cater to the needs of first generation entrepreneurs in particular and small scale industries in general. It will also render specialized service to such industrial units (since initiated by the Government of India).

Scheme of incentives need to be rationalised and properly implemented. Undue competition among the states to be reduced through rationalisation of incentive schemes of various states. At present there is no weightage in respect of incentives for the units established by the first generation entrepreneurs. Therefore, concessional rate and financial scheme should be restructured in favour of units establish by the first generation entrepreneurs in backward areas. Further, there is multiplicity of agencies in implementing the scheme of incentives which should be done away with. Proposed Small Scale Finance Corporation may be entrusted with the job of implementing the scheme of incentives (Central & State) for the small scale units promoted by first generation entrepreneurs.

Raw Materials & Marketing

Raw materials problems relating to shortage and delay in supply should be removed by opening supply depot at all the industrial areas/complexes. Uniform price structure irrespective of location of the area and transportation cost should be introduced. Management of raw-materials should aim at reducing burden of maintaining large inventory by the new units.

The first generation entrepreneurs also to be provided effective marketing assistance through market information, selling of products and Government purchase. Marketing Co-operatives may be formed at district level, market tie ups with large units and statutory Government purchase from such units, timely settlement of bills etc. will reduce the problem of such units.

Technology and Quality

Quality is a major area of concern for small scale units and the units located in backward areas. Very often the products of such units suffer due to poor quality. Quality Control measures are neglected due to lack of consciousness, lack of necessary funds, absence of testing facilities, R&D, and training. It is therefore, necessary that subsidised assistance be given to such small and first generation entreprenuers. Testing facilities to be created by establishing R & D, and testing centres in backward areas. Attempts, to be made to promote co-operative R&D facility centre in backward areas.

Quality and productivity also closely related to the Technology, Modern Technology not only improve productivity but also the quality. However, the Small Scale and units promoted by first generation entrepreneurs are very often lagging in this area. Lack of knowledge and access to resources are responsible for this. Therefore measures to be initiated for modernisation of units through education and financial assistance to such units.

These units are also to be educated about the need and methods of energy saving measures. Energy is a crucial input which is to be preserved and economically used for low cost production and survival. By saving energy, these units will be able to reduce waste and save money. Therefore, energy saving, should be encouraged through incentives linked measures.

Managerial Assistance

Efficiency in quality control, productivity, marketing etc., depend on efficient managers in the area of Engineering, Finance, Marketing, General Administration etc. But, the small and first generation entrepreneurs due to financial constraints are not able to attract qualified and experienced manager. As a result they can seldom initiate measures for quality control, technical innovation, marketing etc. We, therefore, recommend to set-up a "Managers Pool" by drawing qualified and experienced managers from Public Sector and Public Ltd. Companies.

These managers on deputation for short period will assist the new units promoted by first generation entrepreneurs. Under this scheme, it will be an obligation of the Government to help the small units to overcome teething troubles.

Infrastructure

Locational disadvantages in backward areas are widely acknowledged. Financial incentives may be an attractive instrument for inducing entrepreneurs and attracting industries in backward areas but lack of infrastructural facilities are retarding the growth of entrepreneurs and industries. Development agencies should therefore, sincerely try and actually develop land, shed, road, drainage, common facility centre, post-office, telephone, telex facilities etc. Well developed transport and communication system with the nearest city centre is a must.

Poor development of social infrastructure is also a discouraging factor in backward areas. Government initiative is necessary for building housing, educational institutions, medical care, social amenities, recreation etc. Subsidised housing scheme for such industries will be a step in right direction.

Industrial Co-operatives

Many of the problems as mentioned above are partly due to the individualistic approach of the small scale and First Generation Entrepreneurs. He is a person who has to arrange finance, manager production and other day to day affairs of his unit, market the products and has to supervise and manage all other functions which is immensely difficult for him. These problems, therefore can be reduced or removed if co-operative industrial units are formed under guidance of Nodal Centres. Three to five trained entrepreneurs can form a cooperative industrial units. They can pool their resources and take the responsibility of a particular area of operation according to their background. Nodal Centre can play a great role in inducing and motivating the entrepreneurs to form cooperatives and make them successful.

Planned Efforts under a National Board for Entrepreneurial Development

It has been estimated that in India about organisations/Institutes are engaged in EDP. However, there is no agency to coordinate the activities of these organisations. These organisations have developed their own style and priorities and involved in Entrepreneurial Development Programme which are sometime unable to deliver any of meaningful result. It is therefore, necessary that the activities of such organisations be structured and rationalised under the national policy perspectives.

For structurisation and coordination of EDP activities a National Level Organisation namely 'National Board for Entrepreneurial Development' (NBED) to be established. The primary function of the Board will be

(a) Formulation of National Policy of Entrepreneurial Development.
(b) Coordination of activities of various agencies engaged in EDP.
(c) Monitoring and Evaluation of programmes conducted.
(d) Need based and innovative research in view of change of technology demography and social structure.

This Board will assess and develop the infrastructure for entrepreneurial promotion and development and consolidated the base of EDP. Various existing agencies involved in EDP and the proposed REI and Nodal Agency will be guided and supervised by the Board.

This Board will act as an instrument to implement the national policies and programmes to bring a structural change in the Society in order to create industrial culture and entrepreneurial environment, under national framework of economic, industrial and educational policies.

Industrial Culture and Entrepreneurial Environment

The plan, strategy and organization structure suggested by us for entrepreneurial development are no doubt very important but these factors independently will not be able to establish and entrepreneurial society. The success of the plan depends on involvement, interaction and attitudinal changes of the society which will develop industrial culture and entrepreneurial environment (particularly in Rural and Backward areas). In fact, the growth of entrepreneurship in India primarily retarded by lack of industrial culture and entrepreneurial environment. Several studies including the study of Planning Evaluation Organisation (PEO) pointed out that "there have been problems of entrepreneurial augmentation partly due to lack of industrial culture and inadequate local activities coupled with serious gaps in infrastructure".

Rural society is still dictated by caste, religion and superstitions, which discourage mobility, material wants and going for material production. Rituals dominate technology and priests supersede technicians. These cause persistence of stagnation—psychological, social, economic and institutions. No progress can be visualised unless this vicious circle of caste, religion and superstition is broken. One UN document has also stated that "rapid economic progress is impossible without painful readjustment, ancient philosophies have to be scrapped, bonds of caste, creed and race have to be burst. A new social order and scientific temper would lead to establish industrial culture.

In addition to social system, entrepreneurial environment is also influenced by system of education, child rearing and general economic environment. Since entrepreneurial development is a natural process, entrepreneurial spirit and habit develops since childhood of a person. Therefore, planned family and developed child rearing system inculcate achievement motivation and enterprising among children. Reading has a very strong influence on the out-look of a child. Therefore, not only the school text books but also the story books for the children should be specially designed. Steps to be taken to induce entrepreneurial motivation from the primary stage of education.

Economic policy of the country should open up the opportunities for self-expression and sufficient rewards for private initiatives, institute of self-employment should socially acceptable and for attracting young people from backward and rural areas sufficient inducements through incentives and subsidies to be initiated. There is no doubt, that this multifarious initiatives will develop a socially conducive atmosphere for the natural growth of entrepreneurship.

Conclusion

Entrepreneurial development require a socially conducive atmosphere where entrepreneurial habit and spirit can be cultivated right from the childhood. There was no such entrepreneurial environment during British period not even now. Therefore, to develop such an environment integrated policy measures (economic, industrial, educational and technological) to be initiated with the objectives to remove various mismatches like social mismatches, educational training and technological mismatches, banking mismatches etc. This calls for long-term planning under well designed and developed infrastructure and authority with a National Thrust.

There is the necessity for certain changes in economic policy. Structure of economic incentives and assistance to the entrepreneurs and industries in rural and backward areas to be redesigned to promote local resources including humans resources. Since there is predominance of rural factors in Indian economy, our entrepreneurial development model must have a rural thrust.

In order to generate a rural thrust of entrepreneurship development programme and to bring a structural change in rural and backward areas, development policy need to be modified. For successful and effective industrial development in backward regions, regional resources must be fully utilised through development of resource linked industrial complex. Such a development is possible under a dynamic development model which takes into account the resources, socio-political institutions and regionally specialised entrepreneurs.

The concept of rural thrust further calls for restructurisation of EDP and training model which are basically west oriented and based on a different value system. We have to design indigenous EDP model suitable for Indian economic and socio-cultural climate which, would be easily absorbed in backward and rural society. Efforts should be directed to induce spontaneous participation and involvement of people particularly in rural areas. So far our efforts have primarily been directed to plant entrepreneurship and industrialisation in rural backward areas with the help of adhoc training incentives and which in the view of Mr. K. Roy, Management Consultant, is "Artificial creation of entrepreneurs who are to be spoonfed from their birth". This spoonfeeding business is to be given up and entrepreneurship should be developed through natural process by creating an environment for entrepreneurial developing society.

APPENDICES

APPENDIX - I

LIST OF NO-INDUSTRY DISTRICTS/NOTIFIED LESS DEVELOPED DISTRICTS ELIGIBLE FOR CONCESSIONAL FINANCE FROM ALL INDIA FINANCIAL INSTITUTIONS UNDER BACKWARD AREAS DEVELOPMENT SCHEME

(A) INCENTIVES FOR SETTING UP OF INDUSTRIES IN NO-INDUSTRY DISTRICTS/BACKWARD AREAS

(As on the 1st July, 1986)

(As announced by the Government of India, Ministry of Industry, Department of Industrial Development vide their letters No. 4/1/81-BAD (Vol. III) dated the 27th April 1983, 7th September 1983, 18th September 1984, 9th April 1985, 22nd May 1985, 25th April 1986, 28th April 1986, and 29th April 1986).

1. One of the important objectives of Government's policy is to correct regional imbalances and to secure the industrialization of backward areas of the country. Towards this end, Government have provided several incentives to enable entrepreneurs to establish industrial undertakings in backward areas. These include some concessional finance extended by the All India Term-lending Institutions, outright subsidy on fixed capital investment, preferential treatment in the grant of industrial licences, etc. The revised scheme of incentives announced by the Central Government on 27th April 1983, together with the modifications made in the scheme from time to time are as under:

Categorisation of Backward Areas

2. The backward areas in the country have been divided into the following three categories:

Category 'A':   Comprise of no-industry districts plus special regions (134 districts).

Category 'B': Comprise of the districts currently eligible for Central Subsidy minus districts included in Category 'A' (54 districts).

Category 'C': Comprise of existing 246 concessional finance districts minus those included in categories 'A' and 'B' (113 districts including Amritsar District of Punjab).

Eligibility to Central Investment Subsidy

3. The Central Investment Subsidy for the three categories as mentioned above is as under:

Category 'A': 25% of the fixed capital investment subject to a maximum of Rs. 25 lakhs.

Category 'B': 15% of the fixed capital investment subject to a maximum of Rs. 15 lakhs.

Category 'C': 10% of the fixed capital investment subject to a maximum of Rs. 10 lakhs.

(In case of Electronics Industries set up in Hill districts, the maximum ceiling on subsidy has been raised from Rs. 25 lakhs to Rs. 50 lakhs with effect from the 1st April 1985.)

4. Under the revised scheme, the blocks/taluks/urban agglomerations/extension of townships, in categories 'B' and 'C' districts where investments have exceeded Rs. 30 crores as on the 31st March 1983 are not eligible for further investment *subsidy or concessional finance.*

5. The Central Government have notified *71 Blocks in 'B' & 'C' categories districts,* where the investment had exceeded Rs. 30 crores as on the 31st March 1983 in which projects would not be eligible for concessional finance and central subsidy. So also MRTP/FERA houses are not eligible for Central Investment Subsidy for projects in category 'C' districts.

Explanations:
(i) Investments maturing on or after the 1st April 1983 are eligible for subsidy in the specified districts.
(ii) In those areas where investments on ground as reflected in the creation of physical assets, have exceeded Rs. 30 crores as on the 31st March 1983,

Appendices

further investments are not to qualify for subsidy.

(iii) For working out the ceiling of Rs. 30 crores, only investments in industrial enterprises, i.e., private sector, public sector or departmental, would be taken into account and investments, if any, made in infrastructure like industrial estates/areas, power sub-stations, water works, common utilities and services, etc, would be excluded.

(iv) Investments in projects, where approval in terms of Letters of Intent/C.G. Clearance/Foreign Collaboration, Approvals, etc, had been obtained on or before the 1st April 1983, would continue to be eligible for Central Investment Subsidy irrespective of the ceiling of Rs. 30 crores as on the 31st March 1983, applicable to category 'B' and 'C' districts.

Special Concessions to MRTP/FERA Companies Located in Industrially Backward Areas

6. According to the existing policy, MRTP/FERA companies can participate in industries included in Appendix I to the press note of the 2nd February 1973 as amended from time to time. Their entry into the non-Appendix I items is subject to export obligation of 75% if the item is reserved for small scale and 60% if the item is not reserved for small scale. Keeping in view the need for developing backward areas and the role that can be played by MRTP/FERA companies, it has now been decided to permit entry of MRTP/FERA companies into non-Appendix I industries which are not reserved for small scale sector with an export obligation of 25% for setting up industries in categories 'B' & 'C' districts without any export obligation in respect of category 'A' districts.

Scheme of Concessional Finance for Projects set up in Notified No-Industry Districts/Less Developed Areas

7. In order to accelerate the pace of industrialisation in

specified backward areas, specially in 'No-Industry Districts', all India Financial Institutions have also formulated a comprehensive scheme of concessional assistance and other incentives for the setting up of units in such areas. Under the new scheme, the policy thrust is on providing graded scale of incentives to attract investment in 'No-Industry-Districts' and other relatively more backward regions. The salient features of the new scheme, introduced with effect from the 1st April 1983, are given as follows:

(i) New projects in all the three category districts are eligible for concessional rupee finance on aggregate basis from the Financial Institutions as under:

District/ Areas	Loan Assistance/ Deferred Payment Guarantee (Rs. Crores)	Underwriting Assistance (Rs. Crores)
Category 'A': (NIDs)	5.00	2.50
Category 'B':	3.00	1.50
Category 'C':	2.00	1.00

However projects set up in 'Notified Blocks' in 'B' and 'C' category districts where the investment had exceeded Rs. 30 crores on the 31st March 1983 are not eligible for concessional finance.

(ii) The concessional portion of the loan assistance carries interest @ 12.5% p.a. as against the normal lending rate of 14% p.a. So also, the rate of underwriting commission on shares, debentures, etc., is reduced on the concessional portion of underwriting assistance by 50% and the rate of guarantee commission on deferred payment guarantee is reduced by 25% on the concessional portion of assistance as indicated above.

(iii) In Category 'A' Districts (NIDs), as also in Category 'B' Districts the norm of promoters' contribution has been reduced to 15% of the total cost of the project. In Category 'C' districts the norm of minimum promoters' contribution is 17.5% of the total cost of the project.

(iv) No commitment charge is levied on the undrawn portion of rupee loans sanctioned to projects in Category 'A' districts (NIDs) (costing up Rs. 50 crores). In respect of projects in 'B' and 'C' Category districts, as also for projects costing more than Rs. 50 crores set up in Category 'A' districts, commitment charge is levied on the undrawn portion of the rupee loan amount bearing concessional rate of interest, at half-the-normal rate; the normal rate of commission from the date of letter of intent or upto the date of signing of loan agreement, whichever is earlier, 1% p.a. for a period of 365 days thereafter, and after that 1/2% p.a.

Project-specific Infrastructure Development Loan

8. In Category 'A' districts (NIDs), new projects costing upto Rs. 50 crores are entitled to an interest-free loan for the development of 'project-specific infrastructure' during their construction period. After the project has gone into production, the project-specific infrastructure loan which is limited to 20% of the project cost of Rs. 5 crores, whichever is lower, carries concessional rate of interest of 12.5% p.a. No promoters' contribution is expected in respect of expenditure on 'project-specific infrastructure'. 'Further, project-specific infrastructure loan is over and above the project finance loan; in other words a new project being set up in Category 'A' district (NID) can avail itself of concessional finance upto a maximum of Rs. 10 crores, Rs. 5 crores for project-finance and another Rs. 5 crores for project-specific infrastructure development.' Infrastructure for this purpose includes approach roads, railway siding, minimum housing facilities, laying of power lines and water pipes, captive power plant (not in the nature of stand-by arrangement) and other items of developmental expenditure for infrastructure as may be considered necessary for the projects.

Preferential Treatment for New Industries in Punjab

9. In respect of all new projects in Punjab, rupee loan assistance upto Rs. 3 crores carries, with effect from the 1st July 1985, concessional rate of interest of 12.5% and underwriting assistance

upto Rs. 1.5 crores in respect of such projects carries concessional rate of underwriting commission. As regards promoters' contribution and debt equity ratio of projects proposed to be set up in the State of Punjab, Institutions adopt a flexible and liberal approach and special efforts are made to dispose of expeditiously all applications for assistance for projects coming up in the State of Punjab.

Assistance for Infrastructural Development in Identified Growth Centres

10. Under scheme, the Central Government assists the State Government to take up infrastructural development in one or more of the identified growth centres in each no-industry district. The assistance from the Central Government is limited to 1/3rd of the total cost of the infrastructural development subject to a maximum of Rs. 2 crores per district. The cost of infrastructure development is not normally to exceed Rs. 6 crores which is shared to the extent of Rs. 2 crores each by Central Government, State Government & IDBI. In case more than one 'Growth Centre' is envisaged in a 'No-Industry District', establishment of two growth centres per NID can be allowed but within the total expenditure limit of Rs. 6 crores. The assistance from IDBI is provided by way of loans through the State Industrial Development Corporations (SIDCs) or any other designated Corporation. In the case of District in the North Eastern Region, the State Government's share upto Rs. 2 crores can be met either by the State Government concerned from its own budget or obtaining a loan from IDBI.

Setting up of Nucleus Plants and Ancillaries

11. As rapid industrialisation of backward areas would be facilitated by providing an impetus for the setting up of such industries as can promote the development of ancillary units in the area, Government have recognised certain industrial units of this type as Nucleus plants. An industrial unit will qualify as Nucleus Plant if it fulfills the following criteria:

(i) The nucleus plant will have to be located in any one of the identified central subsidy districts/areas.
(ii) The obligations and concessions in respect of nucleus plant would be available to it if it is conferred with the status of a nucleus plant through a procedure of certification

by the Ministry of Industry. On being so certified, the nucleus plant would be entitled subject to performance of obligations, to all the Central and State level incentives.

(iii) To be certified as a nucleus plant, the project report should indicate that 50 per cent of production in the plant would be through off-loading specified assemblies/sub-assemblies components to ancillaries. The nucleus plant itself would not be permitted to set up manufacturing facilities in respect of such identified items to be off-loaded. The conditions regarding such off-loading would be monitored by the State Governments, DC (SSI) and DGTD.

(iv) The nucleus plant would be expected to promote new ancillaries in the local areas as part of its programme of 50 per cent ancillarization. The project report should contain specified plan about the products and items; the number of units and the technology promoting greater employment that would be involved in setting up such ancillaries. In respect of such ancillaries, the nucleus plant would be under an obligation to supply technology, design and documentation, training and, wherever possible new raw materials.

(v) In order to promote widespread employment through this programme, the ancillarization plan of the nucleus plant should provide for at least three times direct employment in the ancillaries.

12. In order to obtain certification as Nucleus Plant, an entrepreneur will have to apply in the prescribed Proforma while applying for Industrial Licence/Registration Certificate approvals to the competent authority.

13. The rate of Central Investment Subsidy for Nucleus Plant is as follows:

Districts in Category 'A'—25% upto a ceiling of Rs. 25 lakhs.
Districts in Category 'B'—20% upto a ceiling of Rs. 20 lakhs.
Districts in Category 'C'—15% upto a ceiling of Rs. 15 lakhs.

14. MRTP/FERA companies are not, however, entitled to Central Investment Subsidy in respect of nucleus plants in Category 'C' areas. Nevertheless, the following additional concessions and incentives are available to all nucleus plants including the MRTP/FERA companies:

(i) Inter-corporate-investments will be allowed on case to case basis upto a ceiling of 30% instead of the present ceiling of 10% under Section 372(1) of the Companies Act. This would be adopted as a guideline by the Deptt. of Company Affairs which would consider applications on case to case basis.

(ii) Convertibility clause imposed by the term lending institutions will not apply to Nucleus plants located in categories A, B & C districts for a period of 7 years from the date of sanction or 5 years from the date of disbursement whichever is later.

(iii) State Governments will extend to nucleus plants composite package of assistance similar to the Pioneer unit scheme in force in Maharashtra like exemption from Sales Tax liability, interest free sales tax loan, capital investment subsidy from state funds, etc.

15. This scheme, which was introduced for two years upto the 31st March 1985, has been extended upto the 31st March 1987.

(B) LIST OF NO-INDUSTRY/LESS DEVELOPED DISTRICTS/AREAS
CATEGORY 'A' DISTRICTS (134)

State/Union Territory	Districts	
No-Industry Districts		
1. Bihar	Aurangabad, Bhojpur, Khagaria, Nalanda, Purnea, Saharsa (including Madhepura)	(6)
2. Gujarat	Dangs	(1)
3. Karnataka	Bidar	(1)
4. Kerala	Idukki, Wynad	(2)
5. Madhya Pradesh	Balaghat, Bhind, Chhatarpur, Chhindwara, Damoh, Datia, Dhar, Guna, Jhabua, Mandla, Narsinghpur, Panna, Rajgarh, Seoni, Shivpuri Sidhi, Surguja, Tikamgarh	(18)
6. Maharasntra	Gadchiroli	(1)
7. Orissa	Balasore, Bolangir, Boudh Khonomels (Phulbani)	(3)
8. Rajasthan	Jaisalmer, Sirohi, Barmer, Churu	(4)
9. Uttar Pradesh	Banda, Fatehpur, Hamirpur, Jalaun, Jaunpur, Sultanpur, Kanpur Dehat	(7)
10. West Bengal	Bankura, Cooch Behar, Jalpaiguri, Malda	(4)
	Sub-total:	47

Appendices

State/Union Territory	Districts	Category 'A' Districts (Contd)

Special Region Districts

	State/Union Territory	Districts	
1.	Assam	Cachar, Goalpara, Kamrup, Karbi Anglong, Nowgong, North Cachar Hill*, Lakhimpur*, Darang, Dibrugarh, Sivsagar	(10)
2.	Himachal Pradesh	Chamba*, Kangra*, Kulu*, Kinnaur*, Lahaul & Spiti*, Solan, Sirmur, Bilaspur, Hamirpur, Mandi, Simla, Una	(12)
3.	Jammu & Kashmir	Anantnag, Baramula, Doda*, Jammu, Kathua, Ladakh*, Poonch*, Rajouri,* Srinagar, Udhampur*, Badgam, Kargil, Kupwara*, Pulwama*	(14)
4.	Meghalaya	East Garo Hills*, West Garo Hills,* Jaintia Hills*, East Khasi Hills, West Khasi Hills*	(5)
5.	Manipur	Manipur Central*, Manipur East*, Manipur North*, Manipur South*, Manipur West*, Tangoupal*	(6)
6.	Nagaland	Kohima, Mokokchung, Tuensang*, Phek, Mon, Wokha, Zunheboto	(7)
7.	Sikkim	Gangtok*, Gyalshing*, Mangan*, Namchi*	(4)
8.	Tripura	Tripura North*, Tripura South*, Tripura West*	(3)
9.	Uttar Pradesh	Almora, Chamoli*, Pauri Garhwal*, Tehri Garhwal*, Uttar Kashi*, Pithoragarh, Dehradun, Nainital	(8)
10.	West Bengal	Darjeeling*	(1)
11.	Andaman & Nicobar Islands	Andaman Islands, Nicobar Islands*	(2)
12.	Arunachal Pradesh	Tirap*, East Kameng*, West Kameng*, East Siang*, West Siang*, Lower Subansiri*, Upper Subansiri*, Dubang Valley, Lohit	(9)
13.	Dadra & Nagar Haveli	Dadra & Nagar Haveli*	(1)
14.	Goa, Daman & Diu	Goa, Daman & Diu	(1)
15.	Lakshadweep	Lakshadweep*	(1)
16.	Mizoram	Aizawl*, Lunglex*	(2)
17.	Pondicherry	Pondicherry	(1)
		Sub-total:	87
		Total :	134

*No-Industry Districts within the Special Region Category.

CATEGORY 'B' DISTRICTS (54)

State/Union Territory	Districts
1. Andhra Pradesh	Srikakulam district and 5 areas:
	Two areas from Rayalaseema region comprising 22 blocks.
	Area-I: Comprising 13 blocks viz. Chittoor, Bangarupalem, Pulicherla, Puttur, Chandragiri and Kalahasthi (from Chittoor district) and Kodur, Rajampet, Sidhout, Cuddapah, Kamalapuram, Proddutur and Pulivendla (from Cuddapah district).
	Area-II: Comprising 9 blocks viz. Tadapatri, Singanamala, Gooty, Kudair (from Anantapur district) and Dhone, Kurnool, Banganapalli, Nandyal and Giddalur (from Kurnool district).
	Three 'areas' from Telangana region comprising 43 blocks:
	Area-I: Comprising 14 blocks viz., Mahabubnagar, Jadcherla, Shadnagar, Kalwakurthy and Amangal (from Mahbubnagar district) and Nalgonda, Mungadi, Nakrakal, Suryapet, Kodad, Huzurnagar, Miryalguda, Peddavora and Devarakonda (from Nalgonda district).
	Area-II: Comprising 14 blocks viz., Khammam, Thirumalaipalem, Kallur, Yellandu, Kothagudem, Aswaraopeta, Burgampad and Bhadrachalam (from Khammam district) and Mehbubabad and Narasampet, Hanmakonda, Ghanapur, Jangaon and Mulug (from Warangal district).
	Area-III: Comprising 15 blocks viz., Zaheerabad, Patancheruvu, Narasapur, Medak and Siddipet (from Medak district) Yedapalli, Nizamabad, Kamareddy and Domakonda, (from Nizamabad district) and Sircilla, Karimnagar, Sultanabad, Peddapalli, Manthani and Huzurabad (from Karimnagar district).
	(equivalent to 3 districts)
2. Bihar	Bhagalpur, Darbhanga, Champaran, Palamau and Santhal Parganas (5)
3. Gujarat	Panchmahals, Broach and Surendranagar (3)
4. Haryana	Reorganised Mohindergarh district (comprising Mohindergarh and Rewari sub-divisions) Bhiwari district (comprising Bhiwani and Dadri sub-division) and one 'area' comprising

Appendices

Category 'B' Districts (Contd)

State/Union Territory	Districts	
	8 block viz. Hissar block No. 1 and Barwana block (of Hissar Tehsil) Hansi block No.1 (from Hansi Tehsil) Bahuna block (from Fatehabad Tehsil) Tohana block/tehsil (from Tohana Tehsil) from district Hissar, Jind block and Julana Block (from Jind Tehsil) Uchana block (Narwana Tehsil) from the district of Jind.	
	(equivalent to 3 districts)	
5. Karnataka	Raichur, Mysore and Dharwar	(3)
6. Kerala	Alleppey, Cannanore and Malapuram	(3)
7. *Madhya Pradesh (six Areas)	**Area-I**: (From Eastern Region) comprising blocks viz., Korba, Baloda, Champa, Kota, Masturi and Bilha (Bilaspur) blocks (from Bilaspur district) Bhatapara, Simga, Tilda, Dharsiwa (Raipur), Abhanpur and Rajim blocks (from Raipur district).	
	Area-II: (from Western Region) comprising blocks viz., Dewas and Tonk Khurad block (from Dewas district) Gulana, Shujalpur and Shajapur blocks (from Shajapur district)	
	Area-III: (from Northern Region) comprising blocks Morena and Jaura (from Morena district).	
	Area-IV: (from Central Region) comprising blocks viz., Bind-Itawa, Khuri-Banda (Binaika), Rahatgarh, Sagar, Sahgarh (Amarmau) (from Sagar district), Vidisha and Gyaraspur (from Vidisha district).	
	Area-V: (from Western Region-II) comprising blocks viz., Maheswar, Barwana (from Khargone district) Ratlam and Jaura (from Ratlam district), Mandsaur, Malhargarh and Neemuch (from Mandsaur district).	
	Area-VI: (from North Eastern Region) comprising blocks viz., Rewa and Raipur (Garh) (from Rewa district).	
	(equivalent to 4 districts)	
8. Maharashtra	Ratnagiri, Aurangabad and Chandrapur	(3)
9. Orissa	Kalahandi, Mayurbhanj, Dhenkanal, Keonjar and Koraput	(5)

State/Union Territory	Districts	Category 'B' Districts (Contd)
10. Punjab	Hoshiarpur, Sangrur and Bhatinda	(3)
11. Rajasthan	Alwar, Jodhpur, Bhilwara, Nagaur and Udaipur	
12. Tamil Nadu	Three 'areas'/tracts comprising 33 taluks:	

Area-I: Comprising 12 taluks (including Sub-Taluks) viz., Ramanathapuram, Mudukulathur, Sivaganga, Parmakudi, Thiruvadani, Karaikudi and Thirupathur taluks (from Ramanathapuram district) Melur Taluk (from Madurai district) Pudukkotai, Thirumayam, Alangudi and Kulathur Taluks (from Pudukkottai district).

Area-II: Comprising 11 taluks viz., Dhramapuri, Palacode, Hosur, Denkanikottah, Krishanagiri, Uthangarai, Harur (from Dharamapuri district) Tirupattur, Vaniyambadi, Vellore, Walajapet (from North Arcot district).

Area-III: Comprising 10 taluks viz., Aruppukkottai, Sattur, Virudhunagar, Srivilliputur, Rajapalayam (from West Ramanathapuram of Ramanathapuram district) Thirumangalam, Usilampatti, Nilakottai, Dindigul and Vedasandur (from Madurai district)

(equivalent to 3 districts)

3. Uttar Pradesh	Ballia, Basti, Faizabad, Jhansi and Rae Bareli.	(5)
4. West Bengal	Purulia, Midnapur and Nadia	(3)
	Total:	54

*NB: As far as Madhya Pradesh is concerned out of 65 blocks equivalent to six districts, 29 blocks are in the Districts included in No-Industry Districts.

Appendices 153

CATEGORY 'C' DISTRICTS (113)

	State/Union Territory	Districts	
1.	Andhra Pradesh	Anantapur (excluding Tadpatri, Singanamala, Gooty, Kudai-blocks) Chittoor (excluding Chittoor, Bangarupalem, Pulicherla, Puttur, Chandragiri and Kalahasthi Blocks). Cuddapah (excluding Kodur, Rajampet, Sidhout, Cuddapah, Kamalapuram, Proddatur and Pulivendla blocks) Karimnagar (excluding Sircilla, Karimnagar, Sultanabad, Peddapali, Manthani and Huzurabad blocks) Khammam (excluding Khammam, Thirumalapalem, Kallur, Yellandu, Kothagudem, Aswaraopeta, Burgampad, and Bhadrachalam blocks) Kurnool (excluding Dhone Kurnool, Banganapalli, Nandyal and Giddalur blocks) Mahabubnagar (excluding Mahabubnagar, Jadcherla, Shadnagar, Kalwakurthy and Amangal blocks) Medak (excluding Zaheerabad, Patancheruvu, Narsapur, Medak and Siddipet blocks) Nalgonda (excluding Nalgonda, Mungadi, Nakrakal, Suryapet, Kodad, Huzurnagar, Miryalaguda, Peddavora and Devarakonda blocks) Nellore, Nizambad (excluding Yedapalli, Nizambad, Karmareddy and Demakunda blocks) Ongole, Warangal (excluding Mahabubabad, Narasampet, Hanamkonda, Ghanapur, Jangaon and Mulug blocks)	(13)
2.	Bihar	Muzaffarpur, Saran, Nawadah, Gaya, Begusarai and Monghyr.	(6)
3.	Gujarat	Amreli, Banaskantha, Bhavnagar, Junagadh, Kutch, Mehsana, Sabarkantha.	(7)
4.	Haryana	Bhiwani (excluding Bhiwani and Dadri sub-divisions), Hissar (excluding Hissar Block No. 1 and Barwana blocks of Hissar Tehsil), Hansi Block No. 1 (from Hansi Tehsil) Bahuna Block (from Fatehabad Tehsil) Tohana block/Tehsil (from Tohana Tehsil) Jind (excluding Jind block) and Julana block (from Jind Tehsil) and Uchana Block (from Narwana Tehsil) Mohindergarh (excluding Mohindergarh and Rewari sub-divisions)	(4)
5.	Kerala	Trichur and Trivandrum.	(2)
6.	Karnataka	Belgaum, Bijapur, Gulbarga, Hassan, North Kanara, South Kanara and Tumkur.	(7)
7.	Madhya Pradesh	Bastar, Betul, Bilaspur (excluding Korba, Baloda, Champa, Kota, Masturi and Bilha (Bilaspur blocks) Dewas (excluding Dewas and Tonk Khurd blocks) Hoshangabad, Khargone	

State/Union Territory	Districts	Category 'C' Districts (Contd)
	(excluding Maheswar and Barwaha blocks) Mandsaur (excluding Mandsaur, Malhargarh and Neemuch blocks) Morena (excluding Morena and Jaura blocks) Panna, Raigarh, Raipur (excluding Bhatapara, Simga, Tilda, Dharsiwa (Raipur) Abhanpur and Rajim blocks) Rajnandgaon, Raisen, Shajapur (excluding Gulana, Shujalpur and Shajapur blocks) Ratlam (excluding Ratlam and Jaura blocks), Rewa (excluding Rewa and Raipur (Garh blocks), Sagar excluding Bina-Itawa, Khuri, Banda (Binaika), Rahatgarh, Sagar, Sahgarh (Amarmau) blocks, Vidisha, (excluding Vidisha and Gyaraspur blocks)., New Sehore.	(19)
8. Maharashtra	Bhandara, Bhir, Buldhana, Colaba, Dhulia, Jalgaon, Nanded, Osmanabad, Parbhani and Yeotmal	(10)
9. Orissa	Nil	
10. Punjab	Ferozepur, Gurdaspur and Amritsar	(3)
11. Rajasthan	Banswara, Dungarpur, Jalore, Jhunjhunu, Jhalawar, Sikar and Tonk.	(7)
12. Tamil Nadu	Dhramapuri (excluding Dharamapuri, Palacode, Hosur, Denkanikottah, Krishanagiri, Uthangarai and Harur taluks), Kanyakumari, Madurai (excluding Melur, Tirumangalam, Usilampatti, Nilakottai, Dindigul and Vedasandur Taluks), North Arcot, (excluding Tirupattur, Vaniyambadi, Vellore, Walajapet taluks), Ramanathapuram (excluding Ramanthapuram, Mudukulathur, Sivaganga, Paramakudi, Thiruvadani, Karaikudi, Thirupathur, Aruppukottai, Sattur, Virudhunagar, Srivilliputtur, Rajapalayam taluks) South Arcot, Thanjavur, Tiruchirapalli, Pudukottai (excluding Pudukottai, Thirumayam, Alangudi and Kulathur taluks).	(9)
13. Uttar Pradesh	Azamgarh, Badaun, Bahraich, Barabanki, Bulandshahr, Deoria, Etah, Etawah, Farrukhabad, Ghazipur, Gonda, Hardoi, Mainpuri, Mathura, Moradabad, Pilibhit, Pratapgarh, Rampur, Shahjahanpur, Sitapur and Unnao.	(21)
14. West Bengal	Birbhum, Burdwan, Hooghly, Murshidabad and West Dinajpur.	(5)

Total:	113
Category 'A'	134
Category 'B'	54
Category 'C'	113
Total:	301

APPENDIX - II

Gross National Product and Net National Product (i.e National Income)

Year	Gross National Product at Factor Cost (Rs. crores) At Current prices	At 1970-71 prices	Net National product at Factor Cost (Rs. crores) At Current prices	At 1970-71 prices	Per capital Net National Product (Rs.) At Current prices	At 1970-71 prices	Index Number of Net National Product (1950-51 = 100) At Current prices	At 1970-71 prices	Index Number of Per capita Net National Product (1950-51 = 100) At Current prices	At 1970-71 prices
1	2	3	4	5	6	7	8	9	10	11
1950-51	9136	17469	8821	16731	245.5	466.0	100.0	100.0	100.0	100.0
1951-52	9500	17841	9141	17086	250.4	468.1	103.7	102.1	102.0	100.4
1952-53	9309	18483	8920	17699	239.8	475.8	101.2	105.8	97.7	102.1
1953-54	9974	19660	9582	18854	252.8	497.5	108.7	112.7	103.0	106.8
1954-55	9145	20190	8716	19328	225.8	500.7	98.9	115.5	92.0	107.4
1955-56	9710	20854	9262	19953	235.7	507.7	105.1	119.3	96.0	108.9
1956-57	11182	21988	10696	21046	266.7	524.8	121.4	125.8	108.6	112.6
1957-58	11227	21593	10691	20587	261.4	503.3	121.3	123.0	106.5	108.0

(Contd.)

1	2	3	4	5	6	7	8	9	10	11
1958-59	12635	23413	12008	22329	287.3	534.2	136.3	133.5	117.0	114.6
1959-60	13063	23802	12402	22676	291.1	532.3	140.7	135.5	118.6	114.2
1960-61	13999	25424	13263	24250	305.6	558.8	150.5	144.9	124.5	119.9
1961-62	14799	26293	13987	25039	315.0	563.9	158.7	149.7	128.3	121.0
1962-63	15727	26834	14795	25414	325.9	559.8	167.9	151.9	132.7	120.1
1963-64	17978	28210	16977	26746	365.9	576.4	192.7	159.9	149.0	123.7
1964-65	21113	30399	20001	28808	422.0	607.8	227.0	172.2	171.9	130.4
1965-66	21866	28791	20637	27103	425.5	558.8	234.2	162.0	173.3	119.9
1966-67	25250	29081	23848	27298	481.8	551.5	270.6	163.2	196.3	118.3
1967-68	29612	31590	28054	29715	554.4	587.3	318.3	177.6	225.8	126.0
1968-69	30293	32460	28607	30513	552.3	589.1	324.6	182.4	225.0	126.4
1969-70	33521	34518	31606	32408	597.5	612.6	358.7	193.7	243.4	131.5
1970-71	36452	36452	34235	34235	632.8	632.8	388.5	204.6	257.8	135.8
1971-72	38983	36999	36582	34713	660.3	626.6	415.1	207.5	269.0	134.5
1972-73	42993	36629	40317	34215	711.1	603.4	457.5	204.5	289.7	129.5
1973-74	53501	38486	50468	36033	870.1	621.3	572.7	215.4	354.4	133.3
1974-75	63051	38958	59505	36590	1003.5	617.0	675.3	218.7	408.8	132.4
1975-76	66375	42799	62302	40274	1026.4	663.5	707.0	240.7	418.1	142.4
1976-77	71432	43076	66924	40429	1079.4	652.1	759.5	241.6	439.7	139.9
1977-78	80698	46826	75706	44046	1194.1	694.7	859.1	263.3	486.4	149.1
1978-79	87058	49559	81321	46533	1253.0	717.0	922.8	278.1	510.4	153.9

Appendices

	At Current prices	At 1980-81 prices	At Current prices	At 1980-81 prices	At Current prices	At 1980-81 prices	At Current prices	At 1980-81 prices	At Current prices	At 1980-81 prices
1979-80	95511	47233	88813	44136	1337.5	664.7	1007.9	263.8	544.8	142.6
1980-81	113846	50711	105743	47414	1557.3	698.3	1200.0	283.4	634.3	149.8

NEW SERIES

Year	At Current prices	At 1980-81 prices	At Current prices	At 1980-81 prices	At Current prices	At 1980-81 prices	At Current prices	At 1980-81 prices	At Current prices	At 1980-81 prices
							\multicolumn{4}{c}{(1980-81) = 100}			
1980-81	122571	122571	110484	110484	1627.2	1627.2	100.0	100.0	100.0	100.0
1981-82+	142916	129815	128457	117027	1851.0	1686.3	116.3	105.9	113.8	103.6
1982-83+	158217	133214	141331	119619	1993.4	1687.2	127.9	108.3	122.5	103.7
1983-84+	185462	143418	166140	128922	2294.8	1780.7	150.4	116.7	141.0	109.4
1984-85+	205308	147816	183051	132367	2477.0	1791.2	165.7	119.8	152.2	110.1
1985-86+	231876	155000	205436	138611	2721.0	1835.9	185.9	125.4	167.2	112.8
1986-87@	259155	161298	229035	143935	2974.5	1869.3	207.3	130.3	182.8	114.9

+ Provisional
@ Quick Estimates

Source: Central Statistical Organisation

APPENDIX - III

Gross Domestic Product at Factor Cost by Industry of Origin

(Rs. crores)

Year	Agriculture, forestry and logging, fishing, mining and quarrying	Manufacturing, construction, electricity, gas and water supply	Transport, communication and trade	Banking and insurance, real estate and ownership of dwellings and business services	Public administration defence and other services	Gross domestic product at factor cost (2 to 6)
1	2	3	4	5	6	7
			AT 1970-71 PRICES			
1950-51	10453	2538	2085	919	1541	17536
1951-52	10639	2514	2206	940	1584	17883
1952-53	11183	2520	2208	989	1617	18517
1953-54	12047	2674	2293	1004	1670	19688
1954-55	12106	2912	2438	1046	1731	20233
1955-56	12123	3229	2639	1095	1784	20870
1956-57	12731	3517	2796	1111	1858	22013
1957-58	12136	3508	2872	1167	1948	21631

1958-59	.	13443	3730	3047	1207	2038	23465
1959-60	.	13261	3996	3246	1266	2125	23894
1960-61	.	14078	4413	3523	1292	2223	25534
1961-62	.	14217	4774	3771	1382	2296	26440
1962-63	.	13916	5175	4017	1458	2437	27003
1963-64	.	14296	5667	4315	1537	2565	28380
1964-65	.	15569	6120	4621	1597	2710	30617
1965-66	.	13559	6297	4735	1659	2773	29023
1966-67	.	13431	6392	4879	1734	2871	29307
1967-68	.	15405	6626	5111	1788	2938	31868
1968-69	.	15506	6934	5356	1895	3034	32725
1969-70	.	16472	7528	5663	1982	3157	34802
1970-71	.	17802	7594	5912	2114	3314	36736
1971-72	.	17724	7785	6067	2227	3509	37312
1972-73	.	16690	8071	6215	2329	3635	36940
1973-74	.	17895	8222	6455	2388	3762	38722
1974-75	.	17599	8323	6834	2378	3946	39080
1975-76	.	19934	8782	7461	2574	4139	42890
1976-77	.	18674	9575	7799	2808	4304	43160
1977-78	.	20828	10274	8340	2975	4503	46920
1978-79	.	21441	11058	9059	3224	4837	49619
1979-80	.	18768	10804	9015	3265	5339	47191
1980-81	.	21015	10937	9554	3358	5759	50623

NEW SERIES : AT 1980-81 PRICES

1980-81	48366	29747	20437	10841	12835	122226
1981-82+	51280	32000	21860	11354	13282	129776
1982-83+	50745	33369	23187	12215	14314	133830
1983-84+	56242	36058	24397	12890	14804	144391
1984-85+	55506	38364	25572	13639	15874	148955
1985-86+	55838	41418	27141	14585	17101	156083
1986-87@	54799	44745	28920	15442	18420	162326

Source : Central Statistical Oganisation

+ Provisional
@ Quick Estimates

APPENDIX - IV

State-wise Assistance Sanctioned by All-India Financial Institutions

(Rs. crores)

Sl. No	State	1982-83 B	1982-83 T	1983-84 B	1983-84 T	1984-85 B	1984-85 T	1985-86 B	1985-86 T	1986-87 B	1986-87 T	Cumulative up to end March 1987 B	Cumulative up to end March 1987 T
1	2	3	4	5	6	7	8	9	10	11	12	13	14
1.	Andhra Pradesh	102.40	190.66	180.62	392.42	274.42	491.88	159.46	315.75	208.65	786.02	1377.34	2976.13
2.	Arunachal Pradesh	1.20	1.20	2.07	2.07	2.28	2.28	2.71	2.71	1.83	1.83	12.45	12.45
3.	Assam	25.23	30.64	26.96	28.96	36.80	38.35	39.28	39.28	50.94	50.94	272.83	272.83
4.	Bihar	18.29	62.68	31.22	118.87	33.11	92.41	28.53	108.17	55.59	157.63	277.23	960.09
5.	Goa	25.04	25.04	19.90	19.90	23.88	23.88	31.59	31.59	47.88	47.88	332.77	332.77
6.	Gujarat	76.27	422.94	327.30	538.90	129.09	365.59	257.86	685.34	386.39	944.17	1758.63	4527.30
7.	Haryana	22.96	95.72	48.04	120.57	51.56	143.04	38.95	124.03	45.22	163.47	289.32	966.32

(Contd.)

1	2	3	4	5	6	7	8	9	10	11	12	13	14
8.	Himachal Pradesh	31.81	36.55	24.67	24.67	57.76	58.34	65.76	65.76	57.10	57.10	334.02	334.02
9.	Jammu & Kashmir	20.74	20.74	21.04	21.04	50.97	50.97	40.10	40.10	64.83	64.83	266.61	266.61
10.	Karnataka	100.15	193.35	97.71	251.34	115.74	347.34	127.26	419.97	138.46	355.78	1094.46	2446.46
11.	Kerala	25.91	70.39	29.26	74.08	75.39	139.46	45.37	105.24	76.38	163.31	361.49	898.27
12.	Madhya Pradesh	101.60	163.37	67.53	165.47	200.33	289.86	193.47	306.95	239.27	432.56	955.21	1705.35
13.	Maharashtra	65.03	463.30	89.04	543.80	117.56	696.59	262.63	1058.88	188.33	1109.52	1222.61	6410.96
14.	Manipur	0.61	0.61	0.21	0.21	0.05	0.05	3.13	3.13	6.67	6.67	13.34	13.34
15.	Meghalaya	1.93	1.93	3.04	3.04	3.15	3.15	7.37	7.37	15.24	15.24	44.00	44.00
16.	Mizoram	1.09	1.09	0.65	0.65	1.93	1.93	2.70	2.70	3.19	3.19	9.33	9.33
17.	Nagaland	1.40	1.40	2.17	2.17	1.33	1.33	6.34	6.34	1.71	1.71	16.74	16.74
18.	Orissa	32.85	99.07	42.44	123.35	113.17	251.33	37.82	114.42	54.46	149.34	387.42	987.41
19.	Punjab	29.73	86.33	46.31	119.17	63.00	122.00	64.37	163.48	95.92	286.37	455.76	1156.00
20.	Rajasthan	100.45	153.28	90.95	173.53	99.29	154.83	148.93	249.52	163.35	288.50	881.10	1521.39
21.	Sikkim	0.36	0.36	4.77	4.77	1.16	1.16	3.85	3.85	2.95	2.95	13.75	13.75
22.	Tamil Nadu	108.88	275.77	121.29	325.75	124.18	406.77	157.54	689.88	99.46	441.57	1086.69	3325.20
23.	Tripura	1.99	1.99	0.42	0.42	0.48	0.48	1.52	1.52	3.96	3.96	16.44	16.44
24.	Uttar Pradesh	85.26	200.88	125.39	251.21	528.51	746.38	387.34	701.05	608.35	967.36	2027.19	3731.92
25.	West Bengal	52.04	157.59	48.18	167.44	52.99	259.30	221.20	464.14	159.21	326.06	813.16	2147.32

| 26. Union Territories | 14.55 | 69.44 | 15.01 | 68.41 | 33.42 | 90.75 | 32.10 | 189.04 | 55.93 | 214.43 | 176.62 | 823.86 |
| Total | 1047.57 | 2826.32 | 1466.79 | 3542.33* | 2191.55 | 4779.43 | 2367.18 | 5900.21 | 2831.27 | 7042.39 | 14496.51 | 35916.63** |

*Including assistance of Rs. 12 lakh sanctioned by IDBI to Bhutan.
**Including assistance of Rs. 37 lakh sanctioned by IDBI to Bhutan
Source : Report on Development Banking in India, 1986-87, IDBI, Bombay.

APPENDIX - V

State-wise Assistance Disbursed by All-India Financial Institutions

(Rs. Crore)

Sl. No.	State	1982-83 B	1982-83 T	1983-84 B	1983-84 T	1984-85 B	1984-85 T	1985-86 B	1985-86 T	1986-87 B	1986-87 T	Cumulative up to end March 1987 B	Cumulative up to end March 1987 T
1.	Andhra Pradesh	107.51	193.80	117.17	213.76	153.16	276.87	189.58	337.44	168.26	362.94	1077.73	1931.47
2.	Arunachal Pradesh	0.66	0.66	0.64	0.64	1.96	1.96	1.86	1.86	1.04	1.04	8.42	8.42
3.	Assam	7.77	10.58	10.81	10.81	23.68	25.16	43.10	43.10	44.55	44.55	220.17	220.17
4.	Bihar	17.21	57.22	16.80	75.68	14.88	58.89	22.16	60.70	29.53	106.32	167.71	669.04
5.	Goa	25.74	25.74	23.43	28.42	21.72	21.72	23.94	23.94	25.59	25.59	259.73	259.73
6.	Gujarat	97.54	258.40	83.60	264.58	122.38	291.39	176.74	532.18	237.82	695.96	1175.07	3291.25
7.	Haryana	12.74	54.25	16.69	972.94	47.50	125.91	29.90	93.97	36.39	130.39	232.17	729.40
8.	Himachal Pradesh	19.98	23.96	27.92	27.92	29.91	33.24	57.70	57.70	52.78	52.78	253.61	253.61
9.	Jammu & Kashmir	18.41	18.41	20.39	20.39	25.13	25.13	26.36	26.36	37.50	37.50	190.76	190.76
10.	Karnataka	78.40	150.70	108.53	216.40	110.41	292.28	90.33	368.39	118.64	299.71	873.89	2036.42

11. Kerala	13.63	57.35	21.66	62.62	30.26	86.62	36.86	86.95	47.95	106.42	259.13	682.74
12. Madhya Pradesh	45.76	84.26	55.62	137.31	97.31	175.41	195.63	284.95	148.60	245.09	717.03	1197.89
13. Maharastra	100.63	386.53	77.22	430.06	80.37	516.69	154.53	723.87	148.80	810.20	915.46	4867.59
14. Manipur	1.53	1.53	0.80	0.80	0.29	0.29	2.61	2.61	3.13	3.13	8.28	8.28
15. Meghalaya	1.88	2.22	3.23	3.23	3.25	3.25	6.60	6.60	8.83	8.83	34.88	34.88
16. Mizoram	0.33	0.33	0.86	0.86	1.06	1.06	2.34	2.34	2.28	2.28	7.04	7.04
17. Nagaland	1.71	1.83	1.03	1.03	2.28	2.28	4.29	4.29	3.04	3.04	15.63	15.63
18. Orissa	38.54	75.11	31.12	81.45	32.95	84.05	78.89	141.58	55.19	148.32	303.16	715.74
19. Punjab	29.21	82.03	31.77	101.48	47.29	93.25	37.57	96.66	42.28	145.97	314.83	770.05
20. Rajasthan	82.77	118.43	83.73	150.33	60.94	126.93	96.01	162.39	91.54	225.49	599.03	1147.51
21. Sikkim	0.27	0.27	0.18	0.18	1.37	1.37	2.52	2.52	4.54	4.54	9.40	9.40
22. Tamil Nadu	95.95	206.67	180.13	322.46	157.60	346.90	110.72	425.08	106.48	445.68	982.53	2670.69
23. Tripura	3.19	3.19	1.14	1.14	0.48	0.48	1.12	1.12	1.44	1.44	13.13	13.13
24. Uttar Pradesh	71.22	135.97	92.08	184.24	99.45	261.16	223.17	418.57	324.74	570.46	1036.10	2256.92
25. West Bengal	38.42	98.20	44.71	129.26	48.24	159.24	42.39	194.95	88.38	268.73	497.55	1476.61
26. Union Territories	7.77	60.93	14.16	67.98	23.68	74.68	18.66	139.08	36.41	133.53	126.69	631.27
Total	918.79	2108.57	1065.42	2601.06@	1237.55	3086.21	1675.60	4239.20	1865.71	4879.93	10299.13	26095.93*

@Including assistance of Rs. 9 lakh disbursed by IDBI to Bhutan.
*Including assistance of Rs. 29 lakh disbursed by IDBI to Bhutan.
See General Notes : 4, 5, 6, 7.

APPENDIX - VI

State-wise Assistance Sanctioned by All-India Financial Corporations

Sanctions

Sr. No.	SFCs	1982-83 B	1982-83 T	1983-84 B	1983-84 T	1984-85 B	1984-85 T	1985-86 B	1985-86 T	1986-87 B	1986-87 T	Cumulative up to end March 1987 B	Cumulative up to end March 1987 T
1.	Andhra Pradesh	32.10	69.99	35.36	73.89	52.99	90.74	67.68	109.51	88.14	135.34	343.07	639.18
2.	Assam	3.61	3.61	2.60	2.60	2.86	2.86	3.09	3.09	7.53	7.53	36.60	36.60
3.	Bihar	20.59	42.64	18.72	33.67	26.72	49.54	32.71	63.48	53.22	100.29	222.09	439.25
4.	Delhi	—	5.03	—	6.30	—	7.98	—	10.89	—	17.12	—	84.72
5.	Gujarat	32.90	64.53	26.09	58.19	33.89	65.42	39.20	74.67	43.08	80.91	252.91	525.64
6.	Haryana	5.80	21.92	6.86	17.09	5.28	12.77	9.41	19.60	8.77	20.35	61.83	165.55
7.	Himachal Pradesh	6.30	7.27	9.63	9.66	16.53	16.53	20.01	20.01	19.93	19.93	95.47	95.47
8.	Jammu & Kashmir	11.54	11.54	12.23	12.23	16.00	16.00	16.17	16.17	26.97	26.97	125.59	125.59

Appendices

9.	Karnataka	18.63	43.40	28.53	58.27	35.26	74.71	47.11	105.54	54.88	113.58	233.80	512.25
10.	Kerala	6.71	10.19	4.29	8.21	9.61	19.71	19.12	35.09	24.82	46.47	94.56	183.27
11.	Madhya Pradesh	17.04	23.94	25.95	33.29	33.66	41.93	55.68	66.75	54.80	67.43	218.08	281.61
12.	Maharashtra	14.48	49.71	17.41	56.66	16.22	57.83	22.85	70.48	24.08	82.97	222.88	657.57
13.	Orissa	12.42	53.36	13.33	52.34	20.51	52.74	22.79	50.09	20.29	51.43	114.72	362.70
14.	Punjab	7.67	22.33	11.59	22.43	3.34	(—)2.98	11.00	25.64	19.22	38.18	89.09	184.99
15.	Rajasthan	33.17	55.04	32.63	53.17	34.26	52.62	42.41	62.59	49.47	73.08	240.03	388.46
16.	Tamil Nadu	24.02	55.26	24.57	59.55	24.89	64.65	28.44	90.83	32.02	97.89	232.54	574.42
17.	Uttar Pradesh	22.38	52.55	40.93	62.45	62.61	92.48	111.35	151.49	132.04	186.43	414.72	644.70
18.	West Bengal	9.35	19.26	11.43	24.91	12.74	27.59	15.86	33.15	24.05	40.38	82.32	190.98
	Total	278.71	611.57	322.15	644.91	407.37	743.12	564.88	1009.07	683.31	1206.28	3080.30	6092.95

Source : Report on Development Banking in India, 1986-87, IDBI, Bombay.

APPENDIX - VII

State-wise Assistance Disbursed Financial Corporations

Disbursements

Sr. No.	SFCs	1982-83 B	1982-83 T	1983-84 B	1983-84 T	1984-85 B	1984-85 T	1985-86 B	1985-86 T	1986-87 B	1986-87 T	Cumulative up to end March 1987 B	Cumulative up to end March 1987 T
1.	Andhra Pradesh	9.92	45.17	25.89	47.86	31.96	59.37	38.64	67.72	49.97	81.02	235.18	470.55
2.	Assam	3.74	3.74	1.80	1.80	1.86	1.86	2.22	2.22	3.91	3.91	29.63	29.63
3.	Bihar	8.12	17.14	8.04	15.75	12.40	20.93	18.35	32.13	28.38	52.43	130.35	208.80
4.	Delhi	-	4.76	-	5.18	-	6.09	-	7.03	-	10.39	-	63.66
5.	Gujarat	20.39	42.11	18.34	38.32	20.07	41.25	24.34	45.49	31.79	60.66	200.41	425.69
6.	Haryana	6.17	16.86	5.53	13.59	6.20	15.83	5.76	14.85	8.84	17.00	50.07	131.88
7.	Himachal Pradesh	7.48	8.17	6.87	6.89	8.56	8.56	12.55	12.55	15.26	15.26	66.76	66.76
8.	Jammu & Kashmir	9.60	9.60	8.88	8.88	12.87	12.87	13.07	13.07	17.07	17.07	95.69	95.69

9.	Karnataka	15.24	31.47	18.91	43.46	26.14	53.64	31.72	69.51	42.32	92.41	180.94	399.33
10.	Kerala	4.17	7.56	3.71	6.57	6.24	12.00	9.71	19.51	17.42	29.52	69.34	136.22
11.	Madhya Pradesh	10.57	14.06	14.43	21.08	20.94	27.16	28.70	35.58	38.35	44.31	142.27	188.63
12.	Maharashtra	10.13	32.16	12.88	41.02	10.63	35.59	13.48	43.10	19.90	57.73	149.49	432.24
13.	Orissa	5.91	32.07	6.84	31.73	9.34	33.94	12.27	35.73	15.86	40.91	70.40	250.91
14.	Punjab	6.87	13.84	5.52	15.57	3.57	10.66	4.53	11.71	12.40	29.84	66.75	144.75
15.	Rajasthan	21.27	37.57	22.02	38.80	23.86	39.30	24.28	35.98	31.85	45.66	184.90	310.19
16.	Tamil Nadu	19.59	39.55	16.98	41.11	19.31	48.70	22.97	63.44	25.33	68.59	394.41	440.49
17.	Uttar Pradesh	15.67	38.05	28.48	45.89	34.72	54.28	54.03	78.03	67.43	98.47	272.78	443.46
18.	West Bengal	4.23	10.11	6.45	11.98	9.51	15.71	10.12	20.87	15.47	26.36	52.81	132.76
	Total	189.07	403.99	211.57	435.48	258.18	497.74	326.74	608.52	441.55	791.54	2392.18	4371.64

Source: Report on Development Banking in India, 1986-87, IDBI, Bombay.

APPENDIX - VIII

State-wise Assistance Sanctioned by State Financial Corporations

Sanctions

Sr. No	SIDC	1982-83 B	1982-83 T	1983-84 B	1983-84 T	1984-85 B	1984-85 T	1985-86 B	1985-86 T	1986-87 B	1986-87 T	Cumulative up to end March 1987 B	Cumulative up to end March 1987 T
1.	Andhra Pradesh	13.98	33.54	25.96	33.54	8.52	56.44	34.12	38.41	26.41	31.21	221.13	283.77
2.	Arunachal Pradesh	0.96	0.96	1.08	1.08	1.63	1.63	0.10	0.10	0.58	0.58	4.52	4.52
3.	Assam	1.11	1.11	4.61	4.61	16.11	16.11	4.19	4.19	6.29	6.29	48.46	48.46
4.	Bihar	N.A	N.A	N.A	8.65	N.A	10.80	2.75	19.38	6.44	17.46	N.A	80.51
5.	Goa	5.24	5.24	5.44	5.44	5.90	5.90	11.96	11.96	17.81	17.81	55.87	55.87
6.	Gujarat	19.44	28.42	21.75	25.67	28.99	41.32	31.39	54.68	20.47	57.46	181.32	364.70
7.	Haryana	3.14	4.93	2.69	5.71	2.91	4.28	2.88	6.88	4.65	8.28	17.55	36.36
8.	Himachal Pradesh	4.69	4.69	6.55	6.55	11.59	11.59	13.34	13.34	6.37	6.37	54.70	54.70
9.	Jammu & Kashmir	0.90	0.90	10.55	10.55	7.35	7.35	1.12	1.12	8.41	8.41	46.61	46.61

Appendices

10.	Karnataka	18.07	31.27	24.42	41.62	16.84	35.41	13.14	30.87	20.52	35.70	147.16	268.50
11.	Kerala	4.18	7.35	4.47	9.62	10.32	14.83	9.13	18.34	9.57	16.80	45.67	96.15
12.	Madhya Pradesh	18.87	19.71	27.11	27.74	41.63	44.44	44.23	48.67	37.64	42.00	192.70	207.86
13.	Maharashtra	8.80	36.00	18.17	34.80	13.97	42.94	14.17	40.26	26.61	60.26	162.18	399.68
14.	Manipur	—	—	—	—	—	—	0.25	0.25	6.53	6.53	6.78	6.78
15.	Meghalaya	1.38	1.38	0.56	0.56	1.44	1.44	4.67	4.67	4.41	4.41	15.00	15.00
16.	Mizoram	0.54	0.54	0.50	0.50	2.00	2.00	3.05	3.05	5.52	5.52	11.85	11.85
17.	Nagaland	0.26	0.26	1.60	1.60	2.02	2.02	1.02	1.02	1.42	1.42	11.97	11.97
18.	Orissa	6.08	20.98	8.88	22.61	9.68	22.11	7.15	10.08	9.98	15.90	73.50	143.16
19.	Pondicherry	7.13	7.13	11.37	11.37	12.52	12.52	12.37	12.37	12.57	12.57	55.54	55.54
20.	Punjab	2.78	9.92	7.53	15.32	4.01	7.89	2.15	12.82	13.44	29.88	69.79	147.15
21.	Rajasthan	9.96	14.20	9.54	10.14	16.46	17.85	17.01	18.98	17.76	22.76	108.46	133.27
22.	Sikkim	0.42	0.42	1.32	1.32	1.75	1.75	3.41	3.41	3.91	3.91	11.94	11.94
23.	Tamil Nadu	19.10	30.55	14.00	39.62	24.31	49.08	25.71	49.24	19.92	46.54	136.65	247.12
24.	Tripura	—	—	—	—	0.15	0.15	0.30	0.30	0.90	0.90	1.35	1.35
25.	Uttar Pradesh	7.13	17.38	15.87	23.20	32.72	42.53	75.24	92.13	50.34	82.34	221.56	315.10
26.	West Bengal	15.62	19.76	14.36	22.77	15.08	25.56	22.36	30.44	25.34	29.98	139.70	202.14
	Total	169.78	296.64	233.33	364.59	287.90	477.94	357.21	526.96	363.31	571.29	2041.86	3250.06

Source : Report on Development Banking in India, 1986-87, IDBI, Bombay.

APPENDIX - IX

State-wise Assistance Disbursed by State Industrial Development Corporations

Disbursements

Sr. No	SIDC	1982-83 B	1982-83 T	1983-84 B	1983-84 T	1984-85 B	1984-85 T	1985-86 B	1985-86 T	1986-87 B	1986-87 T	Cumulative up to end March 1987 B	Cumulative up to end March 1987 T
1.	Andhra Pradesh	9.26	18.55	14.00	22.85	6.57	25.42	9.36	38.83	7.11	24.84	103.22	180.00
2.	Arunachal Pradesh	0.04	0.04	0.91	0.91	0.78	0.78	0.86	0.86	0.47	0.47	3.18	3.18
3.	Assam	0.63	0.63	3.78	3.78	9.21	9.21	6.67	6.67	9.03	9.03	44.97	44.97
4.	Bihar	N.A	N.A	N.A	6.13	N.A	4.60	2.58	7.60	1.12	10.73	N.A	42.56
5.	Goa	3.37	3.37	3.79	3.79	4.60	4.60	5.28	5.28	8.33	8.33	33.47	33.47
6.	Gujarat	10.13	22.02	11.00	22.42	17.77	25.38	21.46	34.18	22.28	46.49	110.86	228.59
7.	Haryana	0.90	2.21	2.48	3.93	2.39	3.53	2.91	3.66	2.88	5.29	13.41	24.58
8.	Himachal Pradesh	3.96	3.96	4.50	4.50	5.40	5.40	11.06	11.06	8.83	8.83	39.86	39.86
9.	Jammu & Kashmir	1.27	1.27	2.25	2.25	3.20	3.20	5.92	5.92	3.88	3.88	18.90	18.90

Appendices

10.	Karnataka	5.91	13.43	3.59	12.68	10.26	18.31	9.51	27.27	14.85	29.41	69.40	146.83
11.	Kerala	2.79	5.90	1.58	4.01	2.60	7.36	5.08	10.25	7.55	14.16	30.88	73.07
12.	Madhya Pradesh	15.92	16.59	17.96	19.43	16.96	18.27	23.48	26.82	18.30	19.97	118.08	128.18
13.	Maharashtra	10.47	28.33	9.60	32.00	10.46	38.19	13.64	44.11	14.44	51.37	124.48	384.48
14.	Manipur	—	—	—	—	—	—	—	—	3.41	3.41	3.41	3.41
15.	Meghalaya	1.43	1.43	0.45	0.45	1.14	1.14	4.49	4.49	—	3.34	—	8.54
16.	Mizoram	0.54	0.54	0.50	0.50	1.30	1.30	2.62	2.62	3.34	3.34	8.54	8.54
17.	Nagaland	0.65	0.65	0.73	0.73	1.62	1.62	1.17	1.17	1.31	1.31	9.10	9.10
18.	Orissa	6.44	10.96	5.31	11.13	6.62	14.19	7.23	11.11	5.85	11.62	38.34	85.21
19.	Pondicherry	4.05	4.05	4.63	4.63	7.48	7.48	7.01	7.01	8.72	8.72	36.72	36.72
20.	Punjab	1.45	8.31	3.60	11.48	4.51	11.70	3.21	8.41	10.23	18.47	59.13	120.15
21.	Rajasthan	12.09	14.90	7.98	9.99	9.44	10.25	10.59	12.47	12.35	13.38	72.64	90.56
22.	Sikkim	0.43	0.43	0.87	0.87	1.34	1.34	1.82	1.82	2.06	2.06	7.33	7.33
23.	Tamil Nadu	10.73	15.77	11.93	20.37	17.20	31.11	15.62	32.23	17.21	35.24	95.60	164.28
24.	Tripura	—	—	—	—	0.02	0.02	0.18	0.18	1.17	1.17	1.35	1.35
25.	Uttar Pradesh	9.02	16.78	11.86	19.53	16.80	32.48	34.86	41.80	49.16	67.49	157.08	213.69
26.	West Bengal	14.73	17.88	10.98	18.09	14.05	20.69	12.63	18.18	17.34	24.55	102.95	154.32
	Total	126.21	208.00	134.28	236.45	171.72	297.57	219.24	364.00	251.22	423.56	1302.85	2193.33

Source : Report on Development Banking in India, 1986-87, IDBI, Bombay.

APPENDIX - X

A Statistical Sketch of Economy of India, Uttar Pradesh & Maharashtra

	Indicators	India	U.P.	Maharashtra
	(1)	(2)	(3)	(4)

A. Area and Population

1.	Area (000 sq. kms.)	3287	294 (4)	308 (3)
2.	Population (Lakh 1981)	6852	1109 (1)	628 (3)
3.	Density (per sq. km. 1981)	221	377 (4)	204 (10)
4.	Literacy (per cent 1981)	36	27 (19)	47 (2)
5.	P.C. of Urban population to total population	23.7	18.1	35.0
6.	Technically education Personnel (1971)	588300	66890	78080

B. Agriculture

1.	Net cultivated area as % total reporting area (1981-82)	40.7	58.2 (5)	59.5 (4)
2.	Net irrigated area as % of net sown area (1981-82)	28.0	55.2 (3)	10.5 (22)
3.	Gross value of Agri. Products (1977-78) (Rs. in crores)	33539	5158	2758

C. Value of Mineral Production (Rs. 000) (in 1982)

49430748	388366	1255003

D. Industry and Infrastructure

1.	No. of factories	96503 (100%)	7151 (7.4%)	15576 (16.2%)
2.	Employees (No.)	7714679 (100%)	77625 (10%)	1337718 (17.3%)
3.	Value added (Rs. in lakhs)	1192877 (100%)	74930 (6.3%)	298599 (25.0%)
4.	Index of Infrastructure Development	100	114 (8)	116 (7)

(Contd.)

Appendices

	(1)	(2)	(3)	(4)
5.	Power Generated (Million KWH) (in 1984-85)	15625 (100%)	16739 (10.7%)	26193 (17.7%)
6.	Village electrified (March 1985)	66.2%	56.0%	84.4%
7.	Road length (per 100 sq. km. area)	47	52	59
8.	Railway route (per 1000 sq. km.)	19	30	18
9.	Population served by a Post Office (1984)	4734	6115	5341
10.	Telephone per 1000 population (in Sept. 1984)	4.7	1.7	11.9
11. (a)	No. of scheduled commercial bank offices (1982)	40787	5122	4003
(b)	Bank deposits Rs. crores 1982	52280	5227	9365
(c)	Bank credit Rs. crores in 1982	35679	2462	8115
12.	Financial assistance disbursed by All-India Financial Institutions (March 1984) (Rs. in crores)	13224	978	2605

E. Income Employment & Poverty

	(1)	(2)	(3)	(4)
1. (a)	Gross Domestic Product in 1982-83 at 1970-71 prices	51119	6085	6306
(b)	P.C. increase between 1970-71 to 1982-83	49.3%	43.0%	62.7%
(c)	Per capital net domestic Product in 1982-83 at current prices	1891	1439	2525
2.	Job Seekers registered with Employment Exchange 31.5.1985 (1000)	24179	2089	2102

(Contd.)

	(1)	(2)	(3)	(4)
3. (a)	Industrially backward districts	360	41	17
(b)	Area under backward districts	72%	70%	54%
(c)	Population under backward districts	60%	63%	39%
4.	Population below poverty line (1977-78)	48.1%	59.1%	47.7%
(a)	Population below poverty line (rural areas)	50.8%	50.2%	55.9%
(b)	Population below poverty line (urban areas)	38.2%	31.6%	49.2%

Note: Figures in brackets indicate ranking and percentage where applicable.
Source: Various publications of Government of India.

INDEX

Agriculture, 34
    In Maharashtra, 39-40
    Productivity, 34
Andhra Pradesh, 22, 24
Assam, 22
Aurangabad, 92, 94

Badman, M.K., 126
Banking, 24, 49
    Development of, 50-53
Bihar, 21, 22

Cantillon, Richard, 3
Casson, Mark, 2, 6, 81
Centre for Entrepreneurship Development, 55
Chakraborty, Sukhamoy, 30
Coal, 34
Coleman, D., 1
Commerce Research Bureau, 40
Cottage industries, 19
Counselling, 133, 134
Craft productivity, 15, 16
Custom duties, 49

Development Banking Centre, 58

Economic development
    Infrastructure, 34
    Since 1951, 30
Economic disparities, 22
Economic survey, 1986-87, 32, 34
Education, 24
    Policy, 124
Electricity, 34
Employment, 21, 22
    Exchange, 22
    In industrial sector, 35
    Opportunities, 21, 22, 123
Entrepreneurial developing society, 109-40
    Approach to implement model, 126-29
    Death of, 114-22
        Early death, 118
        External factors, 119-22
        internal factors, 118-19
        very early death, 115-18
    Developing traineers, 132
    Development training, 128-29, 140
    Emerging class, 110
        Incentres, 113, 120, 135
        Motivation & mobility of, 111-12
        Training impact of, 112-13
        Type of, 110-11
    Industrial culture & entrepreneural environment, 138-39
    Infrastructure, 137
    Location of institute, 129
    Long-term perspectives of, 109
    Post-training assistance, 134
    Post-training follow-ups, 132-33
    Raw material & marketing, 135-36
    Structural planning model, 122-26, 140
Entrepreneurship,
    Alternative concept of, 11-13
    Behaviour of, 7
    Characteristics of, 2
    Efficient & motivated, 2
    Functions of, 4
    Indigenous in western, 48
    Process of, 109
    Self actualising of, 11-13
    Theories of, 2-10
Entrepreneurship development, 47-68
    Development banking institutions for, 50-53
    Development institutions, 53
    In backward areas, 52
    In colonial policy, in 47
        causes of slow growth in, 48-49
    Institutional framework of, 49
    Regional Development Corporation, 66-68
    State level incentives to, 60-63
    State subsidies, 63-66
    Technical consultancy organisations, 58

Entrepreneurship Development
    Institute of India, 52, 57
Entrepreneurship Development
    Programme, 53-58, 109, 110, 122, 140
    In Gujarat, 55-56
    In U.P., 56-58
Entrepreneurs role, 1-14
    Coordinator, 2, 9
    Creativity, 7-8
    In developing countries, 10
    In market, 118, 120
    In production, 10, 11, 118
    Qualities of, 9
    Risk bearer, 3, 5, 11, 119
    State as, 10-11

First Generation Entrepreneurs, 69-70, 134
    Age of, 73-74
    Contribution in investment & employment of, 87
    Education of, 74-76
    Experience of, 76-78
    In small & medium scale sector, 106-08, 134
    Location of unit, 70-71, 85, 91
    Methodology, 70
    Motivation and mobility, 78-87
        Financial institution, role of, 84-87
        Motivation, 78-80
        Regional mobility, 83-84
        Social mobility, 80-83
    Objectives of field study, 69
    Performance of, 91-108
    Size of units, 72-73
    Type of organisation, 71-72
Five Year Plans
    1st, 18
    2nd, 18
    3rd, 26
    5th, 19
    7th, 20, 32

GIC, 20, 51
Gujarat, 21, 22, 24
    Entrepreneurship Development programme, 55-56
Gujarat Industrial Investment Corporation, 55, 56
Gujarat State Financial Corporation, 55, 56

Hagen, Everett, 7, 8, 9, 10
Haryana, 21, 22, 24
Heavy industries, 17, 18, 34
Himachal Pradesh, 22
Human resource development policy, 123, 126, 128

India Investment Centre, 55, 57
Industrial
    Cooperatives, 137
    Disparities, 21-30
    Expansion of, 16-17
    Financial institutions for, 51
    Infrastructure, 24, 35
    Location of see Location
    Production, 35, 36
Industrial Credit & Investment Corporation of India, 20, 51, 52, 55
Industrial development, 35-36
    Entrepreneurs role in, 1-14
    In developing countries, 2
    Rate of, 1, 35
Industrial Development Bank of India, 20, 51, 52, 55, 61, 133
Industrial environment, 15-46
    Developed & backward states, 38
    Disputes & backward areas, 21-30
    In post-independence period, 17-20
    In pre-independence period, 15-17
Industrial Finance Corporation of India, 20, 51, 52, 55
Industrial finance institutions, 51
    All-India level, 51-52, 55
    Corporations, 51
    Role in backward areas, 52
    State level, 51
Industrial licensing policy, 26
Industrial policy of 1977, 19
Industrial policy of 1980, 19
Industrial Policy Resolution, 1948, 17, 19
    Era of development, 18
    Objectives of, 17
Industrial Policy Resolution, 1956, 18, 19
    Objectives of, 18-19
Industrial Reconstruction Bank of India, 20, 51
Industries in backward areas, 28
    Categories of districts, 28-29
    Financial incentives for, 29-30, 52
    Hill areas, 28
    Income-tax concessions for, 28

Index

Investment in, 28
Tribal areas, 28
Institute for Rural Entrepreneurship, 129, 134
   Course contents of, 130-31
   Foreign study tours, 132
   Stages of, 131-32
   Study tours, 131
   Training programme of, 130

Jammu & Kashmir, 22

Karnataka, 22, 24
Kerala, 22, 24
Khusro, A.M., 34
Kilby, Peter, 2, 5
Knight, Frank, 5, 6

Large scale industries, 35
   Increase in, 36
Leibenstein, Harvey, 6
Life Insurance corporation, 51, 57
Location of units, 70-71, 85, 91
   In backward areas, 92-101
      Fort loose unit, 97-98
      Import substitute units, 92-93
      Market located unit, 93-95
      Resource base unit, 98-99
      Tied units, 95-97
      Unit pushed by govt. policy in, 99-101
   In non-backward areas, 101-06
      Connected unit, 101-03
      Non-resident unit, 105-06
      Sick unit, 103-04
      Traders unit, 104-05

Madhya Pradesh, 21, 22
Maharashtra, 21, 22, 24, 38, 39, 70
   Agriculture in, 38
   Financing infrastructure, 40-41
   G.D.P. in, 38
   Industrial agencies in, 41
   Industrial development, 38, 41-42, 71
   Infrastructural development of, 40
   Power consumption, 40
   Road length of, 40
   Subsidies for entrepreneurship development, 63-64, 67, 68

Maharashtra Agro-Industries Development Corporation, 64, 66
Maharashtra Industrial & Technical Consultancy Ltd, 60
Maharashtra Industrial Development Corporation, 64, 67
Maharashtra State Financial Corporation, 64-65
Managerial assistance, 136-37
Managing Agency system, 17, 47
Manufacturing industries, 36
McClelland, David, 6, 7, 8, 9, 10, 78
McMillan, 85
Medium scale industries, 35, 36
Medovoy, A.I., 15
Morse, R., 49
Mukherjee, R., 48

Nafziger, E.W., 5
National Board for Entrepreneurial Development, 134
   Functions of, 138
   Planned efforts under, 137-38.
National Committee on Development of Backward Areas, 28
National Science & Technology Entrepreneurship Development Board, 52
National Small Industries Development Corporation, 51
National income, 30-33
   Annual growth rate, 30
   Domestic capital formation, 32
   G.D.P., 31
   GNP., 30-31
   Net National Product, 31
   People below poverty line, 22
   Per capita income, 21, 22, 30
Nixon, P.F., 1
Nodal Agency, 134

Orissa, 21, 22

Palia, S.M., 53
Pandey, B.D., 26
Patel, V.G., 55
Planning Commission, 26
Pradeshiya Industrial Investment Corporation of U.P., 60, 61-62
Private Sector, 18
   Employment in, 37
   Role of, 19
Public Sector, 10, 18, 37, 38
   Employment in, 37

Investment in, 26
Number of, 37
Position of, 18, 19
Punjab, 22, 23, 24

Railway, 16, 34
Rangarajan, C., 35
Rao, V.K.R.V., 32
Raw material, 135
Regional disparties, 21-26
Roy, K., 140
Rural Industrial Institutes, 126

Say, J.B., 4, 5
Schatz, S.P, 7
Schumpeter, Joseph, 4, 5, 8, 9
Science & Technological Entrepreneurship Parks, 52
Sharma, R.A., 82
Shirokov, Glery, 10
Small Industries Development Fund, 52, 53
Small Industries Development Organisation, 53
Small Industries Extension & Training Institute (Hyderabad), 53
Small Industries Service Institutes, 53, 58, 132
Small Scale Finance Corporation, 135
Small Scale industries, 19, 20, 35
Development of, 19, 36
Importance of, 19
Protection of, 19
Technology & Quality for, 136
Value of production of, 36
Srinivasan B., 28
Staley, E., 49
State Financial Corporation Act, 51, 53
State Industrial Development Corporation, 53

Tamil Nadu, 22
Technical Consultancy Organisations, 58-60, 132
Functions of, 59
Territorial industries, 124, 126
Territorial Resource Regions, 129
Transport, 24

Tripura, 22
Tsuchiya, Takeo, 82

Unemployment, 22, 123
Problems of, 22
Rate of, 22
United Nations Economic Commission for Latin America, 2
Unit Trust of India, 20, 51
Urbanisation, 24, 42
Uttar Pradesh, 21, 22, 42, 67, 68
Agriculture, 42, 43
Backward districts in, 45
Financial institutions, 44
GDP Share of, 42
Industrial agencies, 45
Industrial development of, 44-45
Infrastructure of, 43
Literacy, 42
Population of, 42
Power consumption, 43-44
Power generation, 43
Road length of, 44
Urbanisation in, 42
Uttar Pradesh Financial Corporation, 60, 62
Uttar Pradesh Industrial Consultants Ltd, 59
Uttar Pradesh Institute of Entrepreneurship Development, 56-57
Uttar Pradesh Small Industries Corporation, 60, 62-63
Uttar Pradesh State Industrial Development Corporation Ltd., 60, 61

Walras, C. Leon, 3
Wanchoo, N.N., 26
West Bengal, 21, 22, 24
Working Group on Fiscal & Financial Incentives for starting industries in backward regions, 26
Working Group on Identification of Bakcward Areas, 26, 28

Xavier Institute of Social Service, 58

Young, F.W., 8, 9, 10

DATE DUE
Demco, Inc. 38-293